The *Official*®

Identification
And
Price Guide To

Postcards

Alphonse Mucha, 1898, The Waverley Cycle Company, advertisement. Sold for a record $13,500 in April of 1990—the highest price ever paid for a postcard. *Photo courtesy of Martin Shapiro,* POSTCARDS INTERNATIONAL.

The *Official*®

Identification And Price Guide To

Postcards

Diane Allmen

First Edition

House of Collectibles

New York

This is a registered trademark of Random House, Inc.

© 1990 by Diane C. Allmen

All rights reserved under International and Pan-American Copyright Conventions.

Published by: House of Collectibles
201 East 50th Street
New York, New York 10022

Distributed by Ballantine Books, a division of Random House, Inc., New York, and simultaneously in Canada by Random House of Canada Limited, Toronto.

Manufactured in the United States of America

ISBN: 0-876-37802-5

First Edition: January 1991

10 9 8 7 6 5 4 3 2 1

This guide is dedicated to deltiologists and to postcard collectors, dealers, and investors who cherish and preserve postcards and thereby maintain the hobby and these treasured pieces of evidence of our history and heritage.

Table of Contents

Acknowledgments

I would like to thank (in alphabetical order) Joel Edler of Iola, Wisconsin; John and Sandy Millns of Waterville, Ohio; Michael G. Price of Ann Arbor, Michigan; Fred Schiffman of Minneapolis, Minnesota; and Jonah Shapiro of New Haven, Connecticut, for sharing their postcard expertise and for making their collections available for photographing.

Joe Jones of *Postcard Collector* magazine was especially generous in making material available, and I am indebted to my business partner, Dave Long, for his long-standing consideration. Thank you also to Dorothy Harris, Editor-in-Chief of House of Collectibles, and Phil Scharper, for their patience, confidence, and guidance.

Market prices were compiled from postcards priced at postcard shows, from dealers' personal communications, and from estimated values and prices realized in auctions and fixed price sales published in *Barr's News* (Lansing, Iowa), *Postcard Collector* (Iola, Wisconsin), and *Cherryland Postcard Auction Company* (Frankfort, Michigan).

Introduction

On the Thursday evening before the Windy City Postcard Club show, I walked into the lobby of the Hillside Holiday Inn looking for action. It had already begun. Three dealers were monopolizing the lobby furniture while examining a box of views. They picked the ones of their states for their own collections or to offer for sale to their regular customers. In the hotel room of another dealer the bed and furniture were covered with opened show boxes, and a half-dozen dealers and collectors were examining their special topics for new cards to add to their collections or stocks. In the lounge the staff of *Postcard Collector* magazine were gathered around several assembled tables with another group of collectors and dealers. Talk was noisy and the subjects changed rapidly, but it was all about postcards!

The next morning we began unloading our vans at 6:00 A.M. We wanted to get our stock moved in and set up to be ready for the collectors who began lining up by 8:30 A.M. The hobby has evolved in the past decade. Dealers have begun to specialize. There is enough competition that dealers work hard to differentiate their stock and to present a well-organized display to attract collectors to their tables.

My sales specialty is modern postcards and I often promote it by telling collectors that 80% of the postcards on my table are less than a year old! My area was set up with boxes of views, a section for boxes of topicals, plus postcard books, odd-size postcards, bargain boxes with my "older" (3–5 years old) cards, and the hottest topics, which were displayed on floor-length rotating postcard racks.

Fashions in moderns change rapidly (as they do in older cards!). There's something new every month, whether it be Barbie, Batman, the Beatles, Betty Boop, or scenes from *Back to the Future.* My partner Dave Long has developed the business with new purchases of view cards and we usually offer new designs of anywhere from 5–15 different states every month. At this show the postcards of the Simpsons sold out early. Collectors picked up the new Wyoming centennial, Hurricane Hugo, and Latin American political designs. Collectors were looking forward to the new Dick Tracy cards, but they weren't expected for another month. Many were hoping for postcards of the Teenage Mutant Ninja Turtles, but we hadn't heard of any yet.

Most postcard dealers sell older postcards, but few can specialize in only pre–World War I material. It just isn't as easy to find in large quantities as it used to be. Dealers have learned that it's easier to sell a good postcard than to replace it in their stock with another good card! It's also clear that many collectors no longer limit themselves to pre–World War I postcards. Mid-century postcards are often more affordable and they may be in better condition.

Setting up at the Windy City show is like old home week for me. I know many of the dealers from club meetings. Many of the long-time club members come back to say hello, work at the club table, show off their latest postcards or nonpostcard activities, and just gossip or create gossip (one widow had a new boyfriend; another looked like a million dollars and had become a world traveler!).

When I lived in Chicago I attended every club meeting I could, not just the Windy City Postcard Club, but the Evanston Club and the Homewood Flossmoor Club too. My free-time activities were fully saturated with postcards. My interest in postcards built slowly, but once I'd been bitten by the postcard bug it totally dominated my life—and it still does. My collections of older postcards include Chicago pioneers, women's suffrage, Vinegar Valentines, and Century of Progress. In the moderns I look for contemporary issues as well as tie-ins to the subjects I collect on older cards.

I blame, or credit, my family for my interest in postcards. My father and mother both had many sisters and brothers, and when any of them went on a vacation they sent back postcards. My parents weren't collectors but they were savers—or accumulators—and all of those postcards from the 1930s, '40s, and '50s slowly grew into a large pile in my dad's bottom desk drawer. As a grade-schooler I remember invading that desk drawer many times to go through the postcards!

During our first family vacation to the Sioux Locks, I remember those glorious, brilliantly colored airbrushed linens on the postcard racks in every tourist shop on the street. We must have mailed all that we bought because I have never found any at home. I've since purchased some at postcard shows and these replacements fill a treasured space in my memory bank—a true example of postcards as nostalgia!

The first postcards I bought as souvenirs/collectibles are still in the album I made of "our European trip"—one multiview for every city we visited. That was 1961, the summer the Berlin Wall went up. Postcards showing the Wall itself are now truly collectible!

These early experiences were of contemporary postcards. I didn't know about "old" postcards then—that happened in 1978. I was living in Chicago, and one spring afternoon I was playing hooky from work to study for an exam. That became boring, so I took a walk down Belmont by Damen to see what was new in the antique shops. One had a basket of old postcards. Most were linens and I rummaged through them enjoying the views from all over the country. Then I came across some older postcards. Many were not as attractive because the colors were dimmer or they were printed only in black and white. But the detail of the images was often outstanding!

What stopped me cold in my rummaging was a view of a little village in Switzerland called Lauterbrunnen. I recognized it instantly because my parents had received postcards from relatives visiting there, I had been there myself, and the mountain peaks and valley are instantly recognizable as Lauterbrunnen. This is the village where my dad was born. What was unusual about this specific postcard was that it was so old that it was older than my dad! I studied the details and fantasized about the woman pushing the baby buggy down the village street—"Could that be my grandmother? Might that be one of my uncles in the carriage?"

I continued the rummaging, enjoying the fine quality of the older postcards. I emptied my pockets, buying $2 worth of

10-cent cards (they were all priced at 10 cents). I walked home, picked up a ten-dollar bill, and went back to the shop, rummaging through the rest of the basket until closing time and spending the entire $10.

The next day I went back to work, headed straight for the company library, checked to see what reference books and periodicals there were on postcards, learned about the *American Postcard Journal* (a precursor to *Postcard Collector* magazine), and subscribed the same day, sight unseen. I had been bitten by the postcard bug.

Almost every collector has a story about how they were bitten. (I heard several from collectors at the Windy City Postcard Club show, including one where a Wichita couple had both been bitten—independently—on the same day!). My story continues with an ongoing quest for postcards and information through reading, participating in postcard clubs, and attending postcard shows. I hope that the information in this price guide will be especially helpful to those readers who have been recently bitten or are about to be bitten by the postcard bug!

Overview

A Brief History
of Postcards

In 1869, based on a proposal by Dr. Emanuel Herrmann, Austria introduced the first government-issued postal card. This postal stationery for brief open communications offered a more economical means of sending a message than a letter. Postal cards were an instant hit and many other European countries (in 1870, 1871, and 1872) rapidly adopted them, as did the United States in 1873.

The first widely distributed pictorial postal cards in the United States were the official Goldsmith issues—souvenir items for the Columbian Exposition of 1893. The colored artwork was printed on the "backs" of U.S. postal cards. Pictorial series were also issued by other firms, some on plain, nongovernment, privately printed cards which required the higher postage of letter mail.

In the United States, this disparity in postage between government postal cards and such privately printed cards was eliminated in 1898 by the Private Mailing Card Act (this occurred earlier in Europe). Freed from unfair competition, private publishers offered view cards, holiday greetings, topicals, and artist-signed picture postcards in ever-increasing numbers.

Picture postcards were highly popular with the public both for mailing and for collecting. The craze for picture postcards which began in Europe caught on rapidly in the United States. Additional reduction of postal restrictions in 1902 and 1907 helped more. One statistic from this "golden age" of postcards offers a glimpse of postcard popularity: the official figures from the U.S. Post Office for the fiscal year ending June 30, 1908, cite

Postcard Day: A postcard invitation to Souvenir Postcard Day at the St. Louis Exposition. Color; published by A. Selige Co.; private mailing card, mailed October 1, 1901. Value: $100.

677,777,798 postcards mailed in this country. That was at a time when the total population of the United States was 88,700,000! And these figures do not include the vast quantities of cards collected in albums and never mailed!

Largely due to the many postcards preserved by collectors at that time can we enjoy the survival of so many high-quality old postcards today!

The mass hysteria for postcards had faded by the time World War I began. Folded greeting cards in envelopes replaced postcards on retail racks. Tariff-protected domestic printing did not match the high quality of European imports. All of these factors have resulted in fewer postcards surviving from the 1920s, '30s, '40s, '50s, and '60s. Thus, values of some quite recent postcards are much higher than for many antique postcards.

The 1970s and '80s saw a renewed popularity in picture post-cards in the United States. The reasons for this expansion were several. The larger continental-size format (4 × 6 inches) offered by publishers was appealing to retailers. The appearance of creative contemporary designs of artist-signed and topical cards found an appreciative audience in a new sophisticated generation of consumers. Improved printing technology produced a significantly superior product.

Most importantly, the visually literate public, raised in the television era, increasingly pressed for time, and accustomed to instantaneous snapshot image bits from an array of consumer electronic products, found postcards an ideal format once again! They were concrete evidence of travel and leisure activities, compact for crowded apartment living, and convenient for hurried messages.

Today postcards of all ages are collected—from the current-issue cards found on retailers' racks to those over 100 years old. American postcards published before 1898 are called "pioneers." American pictorial cards published before 1893 are especially rare.

About This Price Guide

The relative values of picture postcards as a function of age, rarity, and demand are the major focus of this price guide. Introductory information will orient the newcomer to postcard terminology. Listings at the end of the price guide point to sources of more detailed information.

When tens of thousands of new postcards are issued each year, no price guide on postcards can be comprehensive. The listings in this guide offer ranges for subjects, artists, and time periods to give readers an idea of values for all postcard types. The emphasis is on American postcards, although select coverage of some European postcards is also included.

The pricing of postcards is very imprecise. No two dealers will price every postcard the same. Indeed, twenty dealers may offer twenty different prices for the same postcard. The decision in assigning a value to a postcard is very subjective. It will depend not only on what the dealer believes the market will pay for a card, but also on how much the dealer likes a postcard and how dearly he wants to sell or keep it.

No price guide can offer exact and unchanging values because supply, demand, and inflation are uncontrollable factors which constantly change. *This price guide offers a guide to relative values.* The illustrations have been carefully selected to show examples from the full range of subjects and time periods of American postcards as well as the ranges of quality of design and desirability by collectors.

The newcomer to postcards will find this guide an excellent orientation to the entire field of American postcards. Dealers—specialist and nonspecialist—will find the price guide a useful tool for pricing items in their stocks. Collectors will especially enjoy the ability to compare the full spectrum of postcard collectibles with their areas of specialization.

The minimum value in this price guide is $1. While many dealers offer 25-cent and 50-cent "bargain boxes," few dealers sort, individually price, and protectively "sleeve" postcards valued at less than $1. This price guide offers values for postcards worth $1 or more.

How to Use
This Book

Postcards are pictorial items. A pleasing way to use this book is to open it anywhere and just study and enjoy the pictures! A more structured approach is to follow sequentially the organization outlined in the Table of Contents.

This price guide is organized around the four major themes by which collectors collect: views, greetings, artists, and topics. Views are based on realistic images showing people, places, events, and things. Greetings are postcards sent for specific holidays; the images may be real or created. Artist-drawn cards may bear the signature of their creator within the illustration (photographic postcards are often signed as well). Topicals focus on specific subjects and may also be either realistic or imaginative.

All four of these themes overlap. A postcard, potentially, can be classified as all of them! Take, for example, an illustrated postcard signed by the artist J. Doe which shows an old man wishing passersby in Times Square a "Happy New Year" while peddling watches for Tick Tock Corp. Such a postcard is artist-signed: J. Doe. It's a greeting: New Year's. It's a view: Times Square. And, it's a topical—twice over: watches and advertising. One or more aspects of such a postcard can be considered in each of the four theme sections. The value of such a postcard will depend on the desirability of the most sought-after aspect.

In the alphabetic listings within each theme section, general categories appear in ALL-CAPITAL typography followed by individual lines for each time period. Specific cards, sets, and series are presented in Capital and lower-case type with period or date indicated in parentheses.

In regard to photos, the postcards selected for illustration will usually have several desirable aspects. For any subject or aspect, relevant illustrations may be found under all four themes. Thus, while artist-signed postcards are primarily illustrated in the "Artist-Signed Cards" section, examples are also found in "View Cards," "Topical Cards," and "Greeting Cards," and likewise for the other themes.

The illustrations represent both rare and desirable postcards, as well as more common, though still collectible, ones. In most cases they represent outstanding examples within their category. The prices associated with specific illustrations are the author's best determinations for individual cards.

Market values for individual examples as well as for the general listings were determined by comparing and compiling prices of postcards at shows, from dealers' personal communications, and from estimated values and prices realized in published auctions and fixed price sales.

Readers may estimate the value for postcards in their collections by comparing them to similar cards in the illustrations, as well as by finding appropriate subjects and time periods and their related value ranges in the printed listings.

The ranges in value reflect the differing desirability of different items within the same subject/time span. However, it should be understood that not all postcards are desirable, have value, or are "collectible." Such cards lacking value are not included in the value ranges. (If they were, all ranges would begin with zero!) Factors that affect desirability are described in a later section.

The figures reflect values for postcards in Excellent condition, used or unused. Postcards of less than Excellent condition may have steeply discounted values. Postcards in Near Mint or Mint condition may be valued at a significant premium.

The value ranges are not intended to indicate geographic variations for individual cards. Most postcard dealers who travel can offer specific examples of cards that can be bought in one part of the country and re-sold at higher prices elsewhere. However, since both collectors and dealers travel widely and a number of publications are distributed across the entire United States, geographic variations in prices are disappearing. Dealers who travel do not change their pricing for different locales, though they may offer some discounts in some marketplaces.

The minimum value in this price guide is $1. While many dealers offer 25-cent and 50-cent "bargain boxes," few dealers sort, individually price, and protectively "sleeve" postcards valued at less than $1. This price guide offers values for postcards worth $1 or more.

The listings, when appropriate, are divided into four time periods. These divisions reflect the most significant breaks in U.S. postcard values, as well as phases of postcard printing and collecting:

Pioneers (pio.) are postcards published before July 1, 1898, both those with pictures printed on government postal cards and designs privately printed and requiring two-cents letter postage.

Early-Century (e.c.) postcards are those published from 1898–1918—the first "golden age" of postcards. These include private mailing cards, undivided back, and early divided-back postcards. The size had been standardized at 3½ × 5½ inches and a majority were printed in Europe.

Mid-Century (m.c.) postcards are those published from 1919–1969. These include the standard-size linen finish and early chrome finish postcards, as well as "white border" cards. Most were printed in America.

Late-Century (l.c.) postcards are those published from 1970 to the present. Now in our second "golden age," the most common character of the majority of these cards is their enlarged "continental" size of 4 × 6 inches.

Values for late-century postcards do not include the *Current-Issue* (c.i.) cards, i.e., those still in print and available on retail racks. The printing of postcards today has wide global competition. American postcards today are printed in many places besides the United States, including Australia, Canada, Hong Kong, Ireland, Italy, Japan, and Taiwan.

Additional terms and abbreviations are defined in the chapter "Common Abbreviations" and in the Glossary.

Common Abbreviations

adv	advertisement
alb mks	album marks; indentation or discoloration of corners of postcards from long-term storage in old albums
b/w	black and white printed card (also b & w)
c/	copyright
can/	cancelled
ch	chrome postcard
cof/	cancellation on face
.DB	divided back (also d/b, div/bk)
des	designs
diff	different
e.c.	early-century; term used in this price guide for postcards produced from 1898–1918
emb	embossed or raised (relief) surface on card
EX	Excellent condition
flt	faults in condition of card
FR	Fair condition
G	Good condition
htl	hold-to-light
l	linen
l.c.	late-century; term used in this price guide for postcards produced from 1970 to the present

M	Mint condition
m.c.	mid-century; term used in this price guide for postcards produced from 1919–1969
mod	modern postcard
NM	Near Mint condition
o	official
p/	published
pio.	pioneer; postcard produced before July 1, 1898
pm/	postmarked
pmc	private mailing card
pre-off	pre-official
p/u	postally used
pwof	proper writing on face—on early cards when it was required that the message be written on the picture side
RP	real photo
s/	signed, when signature appears in artwork (also sg/ or a/s—artist-signed)
SASE	self-addressed, stamped envelope
ser	series
st	stain
t, tr	tear
UB	undivided back (also u/b, undiv/bk)
un	unused (also unus, un/us)
us	used, sent through the mail
VG	Very Good condition
wb	white border; card from 1920s period
wob	writing on back (also w/b)
wof	writing on face (also w/f)
wr	wear

Postcard Basics

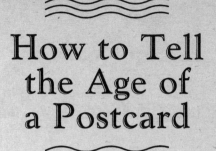

How to Tell
the Age of
a Postcard

As age may be a significant factor in the value of a postcard, pin-pointing the age of a card, at least to the closest decade, may be a worthwhile task. Studying the details of postcards is also one of the most fascinating parts of learning more about the hobby!

Three assumptions underlie most determinations of a postcard's age. They are:

1. Most postcards picture scenes contemporary with their issuance.
2. Most postcards are mailed contemporary with their production.
3. Most stamps are used contemporary with their issuance.

CLUES TO DETERMINING AGE

Using these assumptions, there are many clues on postcards that can help determine their age. The following section (for postcards produced for the American market) offers a way to begin.

Courtesy of Joel Edler

Johnson-Fortnum Machine Works of Berlin, Wisconsin, was the lo-
cal sales agent for Oldsmobile, Reo, and Maxwell automobiles.
The age of this real photo postcard—which can also be described
as an auto dealership advertising card or a gas station/garage
topical—can be identified by the automobiles and also by infor-
mation on the back of the card. It was postmarked June 28, 1915.
The message adds a note of local interest: "Decorate your car and
join with us in the auto parade at Berlin, July 5, at 9 o'clock. . . ."
Rare. Value: $25.

STUDY THE PICTURE

1. What style of clothes are the people wearing?
2. How old are the automobiles? Are there horse-drawn vehicles in the picture?
3. Check the models of appliances and the style of furnish-
   ings and interior decoration.
4. Are the buildings still standing?
5. Have there been more recent additions to the buildings pictured?
6. Are the activities pictured associated with specific historic
   events or periods?
7. Look for details: do the buildings have window air condi-
   tioners? How many stars are in the flag?

Remember! All prices in this guide represent postcards in
Excellent condition.

From the author's collection

This real photo view of the U.S. Post Office in San Benito, Texas, with vintage automobiles parked in front, has several clues to its age: the 48-star flag, the pre–World War II automobiles, and the January 19, 1948, postmark. Not common. Value: $3.

STUDY THE USAGE

1. What is the postmark date?
2. When was the stamp issued?
3. How much postage was used? (The postcard rate was raised to two cents in 1951; however, two other brief periods also required two cents: 1917–19 and 1925–28.)
4. Is the message dated?
5. Does the message contain dated information?

STUDY THE POSTCARD FORMAT

1. If the card is printed "Private Mailing Card," it was probably produced between 1898 and 1902.
2. If the card's address side prohibits the writing of a message on it or allows no space for a message (an undivided back), it is probably earlier than 1907.
3. If the picture does not fill the whole space or has been written on, it is probably earlier than 1907.
4. If the card measures 3½ × 5½ inches, it is probably between 1902 and 1970.
5. If the card is old and larger than 3½ × 5½ inches, it may be from before 1898.

6. If the card is old and slightly smaller than 3½ × 5½ inches, it may well be from the period 1898–1902.

7. If the card is American and of "continental" size—approximately 4 × 6 inches—it is probably no earlier than the 1960s. (But note that European "continentals" date back to the 1930s.)

8. If the picture is printed on the backside of a postal card, check a postal stationery catalog; it is probably pre–1898.

STUDY THE PRINTING PROCESS

1. If the card has a shiny surface and is printed in color by halftone "process" color (little dots of magenta, cyan, yellow, and black), it is probably no earlier than 1939.

2. If the card has a linen-textured surface and is printed with sharply contrasting bright inks, it is probably from the period 1930–60.

3. If the card has a flat-textured surface and is printed with a limited range of low-contrast inks, it probably pre-dates 1930.

4. If the card is produced by high-quality chromolithography with six or more inks, it probably pre-dates 1917.

STUDY THE PRINTED DETAILS

1. Is there a copyright date?

2. Does the card have a printer's stock number? An expert may be able to determine the age just from the printer's or publisher's stock number.

3. Does the card title or description contain a date or event?

4. Does the address side have an instruction prohibiting writing a message? (No messages were allowed on the address side prior to 1907.)

5. Does the card say "printed in Germany" or Austria or any other European country? (Most American cards printed in Europe pre-date World War I.)

6. Does the publisher's or distributor's address include a zone number or a Zip code? (The first two-digit zone numbers were instituted May 1, 1943; five-digit Zip codes were instituted in July 1963.)

7. Is the publisher's phone number listed? With an area code? (The first unassisted coast-to-coast direct dialing with three-digit area codes became effective November 10, 1951.)

8. What time period is the typeface associated with?

9. What time period is the design style associated with?

PHOTOGRAPHIC POSTCARDS

Postcards created directly from photographic negatives and printed onto photographic paper are difficult to date when they have not been postally used. Experts have studied the stamp boxes and type styles of the printed matter on the backs of photographic postcards and have compiled data on the approximate production and usage ranges of various photographic papers. However, information is far from precise, and fake backs as well as reproduced images may exist. For some guidelines on usage periods for postcard photographic papers, see *Prairie Fires and Paper Moons* by Hal Morgan and Andreas Brown (David R. Godine, Boston, 1981) and "Dating Post–1920 Real Photo Postcards," by Ernest G. Covington (*Postcard Collector*, July 1986, pp. 26–28).

Demand for photographic postcards is high. It is particularly important to study unused real photo postcards carefully to be assured that the age of the card corresponds to the picture on the card! Some postcards have been reproduced by private photographers. They should only be added to a collection if they are inexpensive and the image is needed.

What Makes
a Postcard
Collectible?

Condition, age, scarcity, design, printing, originality, authenticity, and usage may all affect the desirability, and hence value, of a postcard.

Just as in real estate where desirability is largely based on location, location, location, one key factor is dominant in valuing postcards—that is subject, subject, subject! The relative desirability of various subjects comprises the major portion of this price guide.

Here are some basic guidelines for assessing desirability:

1. For two designs of the same subject, the postcard in better condition will be more valuable. (In many cases, postcards in Good or Fair condition will have no value for collectors.)
2. The older card will be more desirable.
3. The scarcer card will have higher value.
4. The card with superior design will bear a higher price. Determining design quality is highly subjective! What is considered superb by one collector may be merely satisfactory to another; one may assess a design as excellent and from another viewpoint it is inferior and unacceptable. (In many cases, inferior designs have almost no desirability to collectors.)
5. The card with superior printing will find more buyers.
6. The original card, rather than a re-printed edition, will be more valuable.

7. The authentic card will have higher value if it can be clearly distinguished from a fake. In postcards, the main area where fakes have turned up is in real photo cards. (A fake linen postcard showing a Coca-Cola truck was reported in the December 1988 issue of *Postcard Collector.*) Where authenticity is questioned, correct postal usage will support a postcard's value.

The desirability of used vs. unused postcards varies from one collector to the next. Some prefer pristine cards. Others prefer the postcard totality—where the evidence of transmitting a message adds to the item's significance.

Autographs, stamps, and cancellations may raise the value of a postcard for collectors in those fields, but may not be significant to the collector of the postcard image. The stamp is rarely more valuable than the postcard. Many postcards have been ruined by amateur collectors of stamps who have removed the stamps!

This selection of five postcards, all signed by the artist Ellen H. Clapsaddle, illustrates the range of values associated with postcards by one artist. *All Clapsaddles are not valued alike!* Nor are the postcards of any other artist valued uniformly. Likewise, all postcards by one publisher (for example, Tuck, the world's most prolific postcard publisher) are not valued the same. Of greeting cards, Halloween greetings are among the most desirable; Thanksgiving greetings are among the least desired. The value of a Clapsaddle greeting will depend, in part, on the holiday represented. Novelty, rarity, and quality of design also contribute to the differences in value of these examples of postcards by Ellen H. Clapsaddle.

The minimum value in this price guide is $1. While many dealers offer 25-cent and 50-cent "bargain boxes," few dealers sort, individually price, and protectively "sleeve" postcards valued at less than $1. This price guide offers values for postcards worth $1 or more.

A Thanksgiving greeting, signed Ellen H. Clapsaddle, ca. 1909, published by S. Barre. An unremarkable design; a holiday with low collector appeal. Common. Value: $1.

A Thanksgiving greeting, signed Ellen H. Clapsaddle, published by International Art, #1817. Attractive, happy playing children, a Clapsaddle hallmark, is a desirable subject on greeting and topical postcards. Common. Value: $6.

Courtesy of Joel Edler

A Halloween greeting, signed Ellen H. Clapsaddle, published by International Art. A cute child on a Halloween greeting makes this Clapsaddle more desirable than the previous example. Common. Value: $12.

From the author's collection

A Halloween greeting, signed Ellen H. Clapsaddle, published by Wolf & Co., Philadelphia, series 501. The close cropping of the design, the careful printing with velvet-black background, and the child's lively expression all contribute to the desirability of this postcard. One in a series of six designs. A scarce postcard. Value: $40.

A Halloween novelty greeting, signed Ellen H. Clapsaddle, published by International Art. The arm and hand holding the jack-o'-lantern is a separate piece, riveted to the card so that it can rotate and cover the child's face. A scarce and desirable novelty mechanical, this is one in a series of four designs. One of the four designs shows a black child. Value: white child, $150; black child, $200.

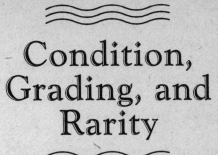

Condition, Grading, and Rarity

CONDITION AND GRADING

Postcards are made of fragile paper. After 100 years of storage and handling, it's no wonder that, even if they're not thrown out, not all survive in "collectible" condition! The following are widely used definitions for grades of postcard condition.

Mint (M): A perfect card just as it comes from the printing press. No marks, bends, or creases. No writing or post-marks. A clean and fresh card. Seldom seen.

Near Mint (NM): Like Mint, but very very light aging or very slight discoloration from being in an album for many years. Not as fresh looking.

Excellent (EX): Like Mint in appearance with no bends, creases, or rounded or blunt corners. May be postally used or unused with writing or postmark only on address side. A clean fresh card on picture side.

Very Good (VG): Corners may be just a bit blunt or rounded. Almost undetectable crease or bend that does not detract from overall appearance of picture side. May have writing or postal usage on address side. A very collectible card.

Good (G): Corners may be noticeably blunt or rounded with noticeably slight bends or creases. May be postally used or writing on address side. Less than VG.

Fair (F): Card is intact. Excess soil, staining, creases, writing, or cancel may affect picture. Could be scarce card hard to find in any condition.

The values in this price guide, unless stated otherwise, are for postcards—used or unused—in Excellent condition.

POINTS TO NOTE ABOUT GRADING

1. Near Mint card may bear a premium of 20% or more over Excellent.
2. A Mint condition card may bear a premium of 30–50% or more!
3. A card graded Very Good may be discounted 20% or more off Excellent—this may depend on rarity and demand.
4. A card graded Good may be discounted 40% or more!
5. A postcard graded Fair may be discounted 50–100% off Excellent! A card in Fair condition will have value only if it is very rare!

RARITY

The field of postcards is so large that it is difficult to quantitate rarity. The following is a relative/qualitative measure of rarity. When terms of rarity are used within the listings or descriptions of illustrations, they are based on these qualitative definitions.

0   *Unique*—the only known surviving copy
1   *Very Rare*—countable in the single digits
2   *Rare*—seldom seen even by expert dealers
3   *Scarce*—desirable card; low frequency of its appearance may be partly a factor of high collector appeal
4   *Not Common*—available, possible to acquire with some effort
5   *Common*—easy to acquire
6   *Very Common*—very easy to acquire

Selling, Buying and Collecting Postcards

HOW TO SELL A POSTCARD COLLECTION

The values in this price guide represent current market prices. They were compiled from postcards priced at postcard shows, from dealers' personal communications, and from published estimated values and prices realized in auctions and fixed price sales.

A person desiring to sell a collection may obtain these prices, *but it cannot be done without considerable investment of time, materials, and money.* The willingness to sort, price, and file postcards; to travel, set up, and sell at postcard shows; and to advertise and sell via fixed price and auctions by mail—that, essentially, is what a postcard dealer does!

The alternative to selling directly is to sell wholesale to a middle person—a dealer. The wholesale value of a collection will depend both on its contents and on who you sell it to. A seller can expect a wholesale offer of 10–60% of the market value of the collection!

There are several factors to consider:

- Many of the postcards in a collection may have zero value for resale.
- Many of the saleable cards will take years to re-sell.
- Generally, the more knowledgeable the dealer, the more

he may be willing to pay for excellent material (and the less willing to accept inferior material!).

- The more competition among dealers—at a postcard or antique show, for example—the greater the possibility for a higher offer.
- The higher percentage of time and investment that a dealer devotes to postcards (relative to other antiques or collectibles), the more likely he will be to close a sale on an entire collection (because the full-time dealer is likely to have more outlets for re-sale).

Whether a person decides to sell wholesale or retail, there are two national postcard publications which reach large numbers of potential buyers. Dealers and collectors advertise in the publications and attend postcard shows listed in them. The publications are: *Barr's News* (a weekly auction newspaper: 70 South Sixth Street, Lansing, IA 52151) and *Postcard Collector* (a monthly magazine: P.O. Box 37, Iola, WI 54945). A national postcard dealer association with an annual directory is the International Federation of Postcard Dealers: John McClintock, Executive Secretary, P.O. Box 1765, Manassas, VA 22110. Send a stamped, self-addressed business-size envelope for a free list of dealers.

WHERE TO BUY POSTCARDS

The best place to buy postcards is in a specialty postcard market. Two types of marketplaces are common in the United States, and a third type is developing.

The specialized postcard show offers collectors immense variety. Buyers can shop in person through millions of postcards of all ages, from all over the world, and at all price and condition levels. Postcard shows are sponsored by postcard clubs and by specialist dealer/promoters. Shows are held at least once a year, and often more frequently, in all major cities in the United States.

Two specialty postcard publications offer collectors the opportunity to buy by mail, without leaving home. Again, the variety is large and there is opportunity for all levels of buying, trading, and swapping with dealers, dealer/collectors, and directly with other collectors. The addresses for *Barr's News* and *Postcard Collector* are listed at the end of the previous section.

The third major postcard marketplace that is developing in the United States is the speciality store that sells only modern postcards. They currently exist in a few major cities, and as the craze for moderns grows more are likely to open. Other sources for modern postcards include souvenir shops, card shops, gift and novelty shops, and classified ads in specialty niche publications.

Of a specialized nature, but still catering to hobbyists and collectors, are general hobby publications, antiques shows and stores, and collectibles shows and stores. These are all excellent sources for old postcards. However, the best bargains and the best unculled "mines" where old postcards may be found may also take the most time and work! These include flea markets, grocery store and laundromat bulletin boards, tabloid shoppers, garage sales, and estate sales.

COLLECTING POSTCARDS

COLLECTING VS. ACCUMULATING

The person who buys extra postcards on a trip, forgets to mail them, and crams them into the top drawer when he gets back home is an accumulator. The person who receives postcards in the mail from friends and relatives, reads the messages and studies the pictures a dozen times, but just can't throw them out (instead they're left on the ledge collecting dust and water rings) is an accumulator.

The person who thumbtacks a colleague's vacation postcard to the bulletin board so the rest of the staff can read the message or look at the picture has just wrecked a postcard! Likewise for the person who tapes a postcard to the refrigerator!

There's nothing wrong with accumulating postcards. There's nothing wrong with sharing postcards. Part of the fun of postcards is looking at them later and sharing the message and the picture with others. But collectors wring their hands in agony when they see postcards damaged from careless accumulation and sharing. Collectors strive to save the postcard for added pleasure in the future!

WHAT TO COLLECT

When a person converts from an accumulator to a collector, he defines his collecting interests. This may be as broad as stating "appealing, affordable images" or very specific as in "views of the town where I was born, before I was born," or "Santa Claus images with investment potential."

Defining your collecting interests gives your collecting a focus. It helps you find your way through the multitude of postcards available. Collectors generally concentrate on one of three areas—personally appealing images, art styles, or artists; places with specific nostalgic value; or subject matter related to other aspects of their life (their job or other hobbies, for example).

HOW TO ORGANIZE AND STORE A COLLECTION

Postcards can be organized by artist, publisher, age, location, holiday, or subject. There is no Dewey Decimal or Library of Congress system for postcards. Nor is there a need for one! Which of the above six ways—or some other way—a personal collection is organized should depend on what is most important to the individual collector. There's no need to depend on an outside authority.

Storage is also a personal decision. However, the first principle of storage should be to store the postcards under the best possible conditions affordable. That includes temperature and humidity control, a pest-free environment, and also storage containers that do not speed the rate of decay of fragile old paper.

Postcards' worst enemies are the oils and soil on a collector's hands. Because viewing postcards is so important to postcard collecting, protecting the cards in sleeves and albums is an excellent practice. However, beware of plasticizers in polyvinyl chloride and other plastics. Polyester is the most inert material—it's recommended by archivists—for paper storage.

LEARNING FROM OTHERS

Once a collector has defined his collecting interests, dealers can guide him to relevant postcards at various prices. Postcard clubs offer a forum for informal sharing of information about postcards. Postcard publications offer ads with items for sale as well as illustrated articles, news, and checklists. Postcards exhibited in museums is a practice still in its infancy, but more professional archivists are recognizing the historic value of postcards.

SHARING WITH OTHERS

There are so many different postcard subjects that each postcard collector soon becomes *the* expert in his subject area. Collectors can share their expertise with other collectors in clubs, by creating exhibits, giving talks, preparing checklists, and writing articles.

Postcard
Listings
and Values

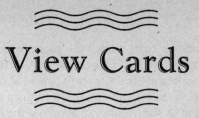

View Cards

View cards are the most widely collected type of postcard in the United States today. Fortunately, view cards have always been popular, and great numbers of views have survived from all periods.

View cards are based on realistic images showing people, places, events, and things identified with a specific geographic place. Most views are published locally and marketed only in a relatively small region.

Most view card collectors concentrate on postcards of their hometown and other places they have lived or visited. Thus, while there are great numbers of collectors of views, the number looking for any specific location may be small.

Because view collectors seek cards of specific places, all cards of the target locations, regardless of their print or design quality, may have value. For view cards, supply and demand for a specific location may affect value more than print quality, design quality, or condition. The demand for any specific location can change rapidly as the number of active collectors changes.

Some view card subjects—for example, railroad depots or trolleys—are collected by subject as well as location and this wider demand elevates their prices.

Most common views, regardless of their age, are very moderately priced—$1 to $3—and can be easily acquired. There can be great competition, however, for the less common views.

Pre–World War I small-town real photos are the most avidly sought after of view cards. It is not unusual for real photo depot postcards to change hands at $35–$75 per card. Values for some of the more bizarre subjects on real photo postcards can exceed $100.

Also commanding high values are pioneer view cards. Even the most common series of pioneer views—those published by the American Souvenir Card Co.—are priced at $15–$35.

While there is variation in demand from town to town and city to city, depending on the number of people actively collecting any specific locale, some general value ranges for common and uncommon view cards of different ages can be offered. The size of the town in the early 1900s is important in the value of the card. The smaller the town, the higher the value. Tourist attractions usually have little value.

STATE VIEWS (pio.) common	$3–$10
STATE VIEWS (pio.) uncommon	$5–$20
STATE VIEWS (e.c.) common	$1–$5
STATE VIEWS (e.c.) uncommon	$3–$10
STATE VIEWS (m.c.) common	$1–$3
STATE VIEWS (m.c.) uncommon	$2–$7
STATE VIEWS (l.c.) common	$1–$2
STATE VIEWS (l.c.) uncommon	$1–$5

In regard to foreign view cards, the majority of foreign view cards found in the United States may be grouped as "tourist attractions"—the most common examples are the Eiffel Tower in Paris, the Tower of London, the Coliseum in Rome, the Parthenon in Athens, and so forth. *Such foreign view cards have little value as "collectibles"!*

Exceptional foreign view cards, however, are avidly collected. Of particular interest are worldwide pioneer and Gruss Aus; Canadian, Panamanian, and Philippine postcards; the subject matter in the listings on the following pages; and first-rate topical images from any country.

Sell prices generally compare with similar U.S. subject matter, though buy offers may be lower. Pre–1900 views postally used outside the United States and Europe may be valued at a premium over the value of the unused postcard.

Scenic view of the Marshall Islands with inset of the Landeshauptmann, Dr. Irmer. The artwork is signed W. Kuhnert. Mailed from the Marshall Islands in February 1905; the stamp and cancellation can greatly affect the value of this view. Unused value: $15.

In general, many view cards may be collected more avidly for their subject matter than for their location. The listings that follow represent collectible aspects of U.S. view cards independent of location.

The value ranges represent the general range where the majority of cards of the subject/time period will be priced, though individual locations and exceptional or rare cards may have much higher values.

Late-century (l.c.) view cards represent material from the 1970s and '80s. The minimum value in the listings is $1. While many late-century as well as earlier views may be found in dealers' 25-cent or 50-cent boxes, if the cards have been sorted and filed by location or subject, they are likely to be priced at $1 or more. At present, very few postcard dealers purchase late-century view cards for re-sale unless the cards are acquired as part of a large collection of older views.

Postcard views still available on retail racks, called "current issue" (c.i.), are generally priced at 20–50 cents each. The majority of current-issue views are found only in their local areas. Exceptional current-issue views, when offered by dealers, may be priced higher than the store retail price.

The listings represent values for general American subjects. The illustrations represent desirable examples within their time-subject group.

For a list of abbreviations frequently used in this chapter, turn to page 11.

VIEW CARD VALUES

AERIAL/BIRD'S-EYE VIEWS (e.c.)	*$3–$10*
Real photo	*$8–$20*
AERIAL/BIRD'S-EYE VIEWS (m.c.)	*$2–$5*
AERIAL/BIRD'S-EYE VIEWS (l.c.)	*$1–$3*
AGRICULTURAL VIEWS (e.c.)	*$2–$20*

From the author's collection

An alligator-border view with an agriculture theme, #S629, "Picking Oranges, Florida," ca. 1909, published by S. Langsdorf. From a series of 165 postcards numbered S500 to S664. Alligator-border cards have an avid following. Value: $25.

Remember! All prices in this guide represent postcards in *Excellent* condition.

Real photo	$5–$40
AGRICULTURAL VIEWS (m.c.)	$1–$10
AGRICULTURAL VIEWS (l.c.)	$1–$5
AIRCRAFT (e.c.)	$5–$20
Real photo	$10–$40
AIRCRAFT (m.c.)	$2–$5
AIRCRAFT (l.c.)	$1–$3
AIRPORTS (m.c.)	$2–$5
AIRPORTS (l.c.)	$1–$3
p/ALBERTYPE (pmc)	$10–$20
p/ALBERTYPE (hand-colored)	$5–$25
p/ALBERTYPE (sepia, b & w)	$2–$5
ALLIGATOR BORDER, p/Langsdorf	$25–$40
AMUSEMENT PARKS (e.c.)	$3–$25
Real photo	$10–$75
AMUSEMENT PARKS (m.c.)	$3–$10
AMUSEMENT PARKS (l.c.)	$2–$6
ANIMAL LIFE (e.c.)	$1–$10
Real photo	$2–$10
ANIMAL LIFE (m.c.)	$2–$10
ANIMAL LIFE (l.c.)	$1–$2
AUTOMOBILES (e.c., nonadvertising)	$3–$20
Advertising	$10–$75
Real photo	$5–$50
AUTOMOBILES (m.c.)	$2–$10
AUTOMOBILES (l.c.)	$1–$5
BANKS (e.c.)	$2–$10
Real photo	$7–$25
BANKS (m.c.)	$1–$10
BANKS (l.c.)	$1–$5
BREWERIES (e.c.)	$8–$25
Real photo	$10–$80
BREWERIES (m.c.)	$3–$20
BREWERIES (l.c.)	$1–$8
BRIDGES (e.c.)	$1–$5
Real photo	$2–$8
BRIDGES (m.c.)	$2–$5
BRIDGES (l.c.)	$1–$2

BUSES/BUS DEPOTS (e.c., bus)	$3–$30
Depot	$2–$10
Real photo	$5–$40
BUSES/BUS DEPOTS (m.c.)	$2–$20

Courtesy of Joel Edler

Greyhound Bus Depot and Wayne Theatre, Wooster, Ohio. Publisher Curt Teich's stock number 4B107-N indicates that the view was issued in the early 1930s. Value: $8.

BUSES/BUS DEPOTS (l.c.)	$1–$5
CAPITOLS (e.c.)	$3–$6

From the author's collection

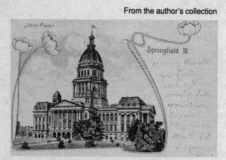

View of state capitol in Springfield, Illinois, surrounded by Art Nouveau decoration; #137, published by Geo. Coldeway of Springfield, printed in Germany. An undivided back card, mailed in 1906; the sender was required to write the message on the picture side of the card. Scarce. Value: $8.

Real photo	$8–$15
p/BOSSELMAN	$3–$4
p/ILLUSTRATED, flat	$3–$4
p/ILLUSTRATED, embossed/gold	$4–$5
p/KROPP	$12–$15

p/LANGSDORF $6–$8

p/TUCK, Oilette $5–$6

From the author's collection

State capitol in Jackson, Mississippi. From the Tuck "Oilette" state capitols series, a widely collected series of state capitol postcards; many are found unused. Undivided back. Value: $6.

p/WHELOCK $3–$4

CAPITOLS (m.c.) $1–$5

CAPITOLS (l.c.) $1–$2

From the author's collection

Charleston, West Virginia, state capitol on the Kanawha River during the Sternwheel Regatta Festival. Published by Cards Unlimited. A current-issue card. Value: $25–$50

CAROUSELS (e.c.) $5–$10

Real photo $10–$30

CAROUSELS (m.c.) $5–$20

CAROUSELS (l.c.) $1–$10

CHILDREN (e.c.) $2–$20

Real photo $2–$20

CHILDREN (m.c.) $1–$10

CHILDREN (l.c.)	$1–$3
CHURCHES (e.c.)	$1–$10

Private mailing card of Christ's Church of Alexandria, Virginia, which was reached by the Washington, Alexandria, and Mt. Vernon Railway; the round trip cost 25 cents. Value: $10.

Real photo	$2–$10
CHURCHES (m.c.)	$1–$3
CHURCHES (l.c.)	$1–$2
COURTHOUSES (e.c.)	$3–$10
Real photo	$5–$10
COURTHOUSES (m.c.)	$2–$5

The elegant and imposing courthouse structure in Crawfordsville, Indiana. This crudely printed "white border" card shows a mixture of automobiles and horse-drawn vehicles. Divided back, postally used 1928, published by Harry Hamm of Toledo and printed by Curt Teich. Value: $3.

COURTHOUSES (l.c.)	$1–$3
COVERED BRIDGES (e.c.)	$1–$5
Real photo	$5–$20
COVERED BRIDGES (m.c.)	$1–$5
COVERED BRIDGES (l.c.)	$1–$3

DAIRIES (e.c.) $5–$10
   Real photo $5–$20

Courtesy of Joel Edler

The creamery, showing horse-drawn vehicles at Cedarville, Illinois. A real photo card, published by the Gem Photo Co., Pearl City, Illinois. Value: $20.

DAIRIES (m.c.)	$2–$10
DAIRIES (l.c.)	$1–$5
DAMS (e.c.)	$1–$5
Real photo	$2–$20
DAMS (m.c.)	$1–$5
DAMS (l.c.)	$1–$3
p/DETROIT (pmc)	$10–$35
p/DETROIT (other views)	$1–$15
DISASTERS (e.c.)	$3–$20
Real photo	$5–$20
DISASTERS (m.c.)	$2–$10
DISASTERS (l.c.)	$1–$3
FACTORIES (e.c.)	$3–$20
Real photo	$5–$30
FACTORIES (m.c.)	$2–$10
FACTORIES (l.c.)	$1–$3

The minimum value in this price guide is $1. While many dealers offer 25-cent and 50-cent "bargain boxes," few dealers sort, individually price, and protectively "sleeve" postcards valued at less than $1. This price guide offers values for postcards worth $1 or more.

FAIRS/FESTIVALS (e.c.)	$3–$10
Real photo	$5–$25
FAIRS/FESTIVALS (m.c.)	$2–$10
FAIRS/FESTIVALS (l.c.)	$1–$5
FAMOUS PEOPLE'S HOMES (e.c.)	$1–$10
Real photo	$2–$10
FAMOUS PEOPLE'S HOMES (m.c.)	$1–$3

From the author's collection

From the popular category, Famous People's Homes, the ranch home of Clark Gable. A linen-surface card, published by Curt Teich of Chicago in 1941. Value: $3.

FAMOUS PEOPLE'S HOMES (l.c.)	$1–$2
FERRIES (e.c.)	$3–$10
Real photo	$5–$20
FERRIES (m.c.)	$2–$5
FERRIES (l.c.)	$1–$2
FIRE ENGINES/FIRE HOUSES (e.c., horse-drawn)	
	$8–$40
Motorized vehicle	$5–$15
No vehicle	$3–$10

From the author's collection

The Central fire station and apparatus, Meadville, Pennsylvania. Circa 1910. Value: $10.

Real photo	$10–$50
FIRE ENGINES/FIRE HOUSES (m.c.)	$3–$8
FIRE ENGINES/FIRE HOUSES (l.c.)	$1–$4
GARAGES/GAS STATIONS (e.c.)	$2–$10
Real photo	$8–$50
GARAGES/GAS STATIONS (m.c.)	$2–$10
GARAGES/GAS STATIONS (l.c.)	$1–$3
p/HAMMON (e.c.)	$2–$8
HARBORS (e.c.)	$2–$5
Real photo	$3–$10
HARBORS (m.c.)	$1–$5
HARBORS (l.c.)	$1–$3
HIGHWAYS (e.c.)	$1–$5
Real photo	$2–$10
HIGHWAYS (m.c.)	$1–$5
HIGHWAYS (l.c.)	$1–$3
HORSE-DRAWN COMMERCIAL VEHICLES (e.c.)	
	$5–$20
Real photo	$10–$100
HORSES/HORSE-DRAWN, NONCOMMERCIAL (e.c.)	
	$1–$5
Real photo	$3–$10
HOTELS/MOTELS (pio.)	$10–$30

"Gruss Aus" postcard of the resort hotel at Rigi, Switzerland. Postally used from Rigi in 1894 to Düsseldorf. Printed in brown monotone. Value: $20.

HOTELS/MOTELS (e.c.)   *$3–$10*

The Great Southern Hotel, Gulfport, Mississippi. Unused private mailing card. Printed in color. Value: $10.

Real photo	*$3–$20*
HOTELS/MOTELS (m.c.)	*$1–$5*
HOTELS/MOTELS (l.c.)	*$1–$2*
p/KOEHLER (hold-to-light)	*$20–$50*
"Fighting the flames," #1606L	*$80–$100*
p/KOEHLER (other views)	*$2–$10*
p/LANGSDORF (alligator border)	*$25–$40*
p/LANGSDORF (shell border)	*$8–$12*
LARGE LETTERS (e.c.)	*$1–$5*
Real photo	*$5–$10*
LARGE LETTERS (m.c.)	*$1–$2*

Large-letter linen of Punxsutawney, Pennsylvania, showing a ground hog. Published in 1942 by Minsky Bros. of Pittsburgh; printed by Curt Teich. Over 1,000 American cities were portrayed on large-letter linen postcards in the 1940s and '50s. Each letter in a locale's name shows a view of a different building or monument. Punxsutawney, Pennsylvania, is one of the most highly valued LLLs because other Ground Hog-Day greetings are very rare. Value: $20; most LLLs value: less than $2.

LIBRARIES (e.c.)	$1–$5
Real photo	$2–$10
LIBRARIES (m.c.)	$1–$3
LIBRARIES (l.c.)	$1–$2
LIGHTHOUSES (e.c.)	$2–$10
Real photo	$2–$10
LIGHTHOUSES (m.c.)	$1–$3
LIGHTHOUSES (l.c.)	$1–$2
MAIN STREETS (e.c.)	$3–$10

From the author's collection

A die-cut hold-to-light view of State Street, north from Adams Street, Chicago, Illinois. Published by Jos. Koehler, ca. 1909; one of a series of 113 hold-to-light views of eleven American cities and locales. Value: $50.

Real photo	$5–$25
MAIN STREETS (m.c.)	$2–$5
MAIN STREETS (l.c.)	$1–$3
MAPS (e.c.)	$1–$5
MAPS (m.c.)	$1–$3
MAPS (l.c.)	$1–$2
MILITARY BASES (e.c.)	$1–$10
Real photo	$3–$10
MILITARY BASES (m.c.)	$1–$3
MILITARY BASES (l.c.)	$1
MILITARY PERSONNEL/VEHICLES (e.c.)	$3–$8
Real photo	$3–$20
MILITARY PERSONNEL/VEHICLES (m.c.)	$1–$5
MILITARY PERSONNEL/VEHICLES (l.c.)	$1–$2
p/MITCHELL (pmc)	$5–$10
p/MITCHELL (other views)	$1–$5
MONUMENTS/STATUARY (e.c.)	$1–$3
Real photo	$2–$10

MONUMENTS/STATUARY (m.c.)	$1–$5
MONUMENTS/STATUARY (l.c.)	$1–$2
MOTORCYCLES (e.c.)	$5–$20
Real photo	$15–$50

Courtesy of Fred Schiffman

A real photo card of Indians (the motorcycles) at Fergus Falls, Minnesota, published by Oxley. The detail-filled view shows not just motorcycles but their owners or admirers, plus store fronts and circus advertising. Value: $40.

MOTORCYCLES (m.c.)	$3–$35
MOTORCYCLES (l.c.)	$2–$8
MOTORIZED COMMERCIAL VEHICLES (e.c.)	$5–$35
Real photo	$8–$50
MOTORIZED COMMERCIAL VEHICLES (m.c.)	$2–$10
MOTORIZED COMMERCIAL VEHICLES (l.c.)	$1–$5
MOUNTAINS (e.c.)	$1–$2
Real photo	$1–$5
MOUNTAINS (m.c.)	$1–$2
MOUNTAINS (l.c.)	$1–$2
OCEANLINERS (pio., p/American Souvenir)	$20–$35
OCEANLINERS (e.c.)	$3–$10
Titanic	$20–$50
Real photo (except Titanic)	$5–$15
OCEANLINERS (m.c.)	$2–$10
OCEANLINERS (l.c.)	$1–$6
OFFICE BUILDINGS (pio.)	$5–$10
OFFICE BUILDINGS (e.c.)	$1–$3
Real photo	$5–$8
OFFICE BUILDINGS (m.c.)	$1–$2

OFFICE BUILDINGS (l.c.)	$1–$2
PARADES (e.c.)	$3–$5
Real photo	$5–$20
PARADES (m.c.)	$1–$3
PARADES (l.c.)	$1–$2
PARKS (all periods)	$1–$2
PEOPLE WORKING/PROFESSIONS (e.c.)	$1–$5

From the author's collection

Mat weaver, Hawaiian Islands. Early postally used cards from Hawaii may have high values because of their postmark and cancellation rather than for their image. Unused, divided back, ca. 1910. Value: $6.

From the author's collection

"Life Saving Station and Crew, Salisbury Beach, Mass.," #607, published by Moore & Gibson Co., New York, printed in Germany. Value: $6.

Remember! All prices in this guide represent postcards in *Excellent* condition.

Real photo $5–$20

Courtesy of Joel Edler

Swendson mill interior, Echo, Wisconsin. Pre–World War I divided back, unused real photo on NOKO paper. Value: $25.

PEOPLE WORKING/PROFESSIONS (m.c.)	$2–$10
PEOPLE WORKING/PROFESSIONS (l.c.)	$1–$3
PERFORMERS/ENTERTAINERS (e.c.)	$3–$7
Real photo (autographs may alter the value and should be treated as autographs)	
	$5–$15
PERFORMERS/ENTERTAINERS (m.c.)	$2–$5
PERFORMERS/ENTERTAINERS (l.c.)	$1–$5
PLANTLIFE (e.c.)	$1–$5
Real photo	$1–$5
PLANTLIFE (m.c.)	$1–$5
PLANTLIFE (l.c.)	$1
POLICE-RELATED (e.c.)	$1–$10
Real photo	$3–$20
POLICE-RELATED (m.c.)	$1–$3
POLICE-RELATED (l.c.)	$1–$2
POST OFFICES (e.c.)	$1–$3
With horse-drawn vehicle	$5–$20
Real photo	$3–$10
POST OFFICES (m.c.)	$1–$3
POST OFFICES (l.c.)	$1–$3
PRESIDENTS' HOMES, p/Tuck, Oilette	$3–$5
PRISONS (e.c.)	$3–$20
Interiors	$5–$30
Real photo	$3–$30
PRISONS (m.c.)	$1–$5
PRISONS (l.c.)	$1–$2

RAILROAD DEPOTS (e.c.)	$3–$20
Real photo	$15–$80
RAILROAD DEPOTS (m.c.)	$1–$5
RAILROAD DEPOTS (l.c.)	$1–$3
RAILROADS/TRAINS (e.c.)	$2–$20
Real photo	$3–$25

Courtesy of Joel Edler

"Depot scene, 1908, Colfax, Wis." Postally used 1909. Real photo #1 published by B. H. Dingman of Plymouth, Wisconsin. The clarity and angle of this small-town depot plus the action of people waiting as the Wisconsin Central steams into the station makes this an excellent depot view. Value: $40.

RAILROADS/TRAINS (m.c.)	$1–$5
RAILROADS/TRAINS (l.c.)	$1–$3
RESTAURANTS (e.c.)	$3–$20
Real photo	$5–$25
RESTAURANTS (m.c.)	$3–$15
Diners	$20–$30
RESTAURANTS (l.c.)	$1–$3
RIVERBOATS (e.c.)	$2–$10
Real photo	$7–$20

The minimum value in this price guide is $1. While many dealers offer 25-cent and 50-cent "bargain boxes," few dealers sort, individually price, and protectively "sleeve" postcards valued at less than $1. This price guide offers values for postcards worth $1 or more.

RIVERBOATS (m.c.)	$1–$4
RIVERBOATS (l.c.)	$1–$3
RIVERS (all periods)	$1–$3
ROCK FORMATIONS (all periods)	$1–$3
p/ROTOGRAPH (e.c.)	$3–$20
SCENIC (all periods)	$1–$3
SCHOOLS (e.c.)	$3–$5

Courtesy of Fred Schiffman

View of Decorah High School, Decorah, Iowa, with artist-drawn cheerleader. The combination of photograph and illustration incorporated into one design adds to the card's appeal. Published by Brunt & Parman. Value: $8.

Real photo	$5–$25
SCHOOLS (m.c.)	$1–$2
SCHOOLS (l.c.)	$1–$2
SKYLINES (pio.)	$5–$15
SKYLINES (e.c.)	$2–$10
Real photo	$3–$15
SKYLINES (m.c.)	$2–$5
SKYLINES (l.c.)	$1

Remember! All prices in this guide represent postcards in *Excellent* condition.

SPORTS-RELATED (e.c.)	*$2–$10*
Real photo	*$3–$30*

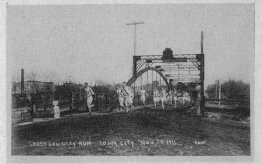

"Cross country run, Iowa City, Nov. 25, 1911." Unused real photo on AZO paper, with photographer credit, Kant. Value: $15.

SPORTS-RELATED (m.c.)	*$2–$10*
SPORTS-RELATED (l.c.)	*$1–$5*
STADIUMS/ARENAS (e.c., professional baseball)	
	$15–$40
College	*$2–$5*
Real photo	*$20–$50*
STADIUMS/ARENAS (m.c.)	*$3–$20*

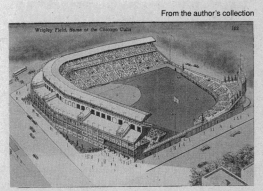

Wrigley Field, home of the Chicago Cubs. A linen view published in 1939 by J. O. Stoll Co., printed by Curt Teich. Value: $15.

STADIUMS/ARENAS (l.c.)	$2–$10
STORE INTERIORS (e.c.)	$5–$35
Real photo	$15–$75

Courtesy of Joel Edler

M. A. Wood's store in Almond, Wisconsin, postally used 1913, a Hanson real photo. The clarity and detail of this small-town store interior make this a highly desirable card. Value: $50.

STORE INTERIORS (m.c.)	$1–$20
STORE INTERIORS (l.c.)	$1–$5
STORES/MALLS/MARKETS (e.c.)	$3–$15
Real photo	$3–$20
STORES/MALLS/MARKETS (m.c.)	$1–$5

From the author's collection

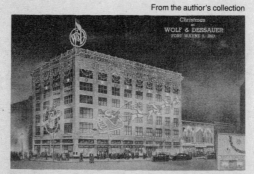

The Wolf & Dessaurer department store in Fort Wayne, Indiana, decorated for Christmas 1946. Linen view published in 1946 by Curt Teich. Value: $8.

STORES/MALLS/MARKETS (l.c.)	$1–$2
THEATERS (e.c.)	$2–$20
Real photo	$5–$40
THEATERS (m.c.)	$1–$10
THEATERS (l.c.)	$1–$3
TROLLEYS (e.c.)	$3–$12
Real photo	$10–$30
TROLLEYS (m.c.)	$1–$8
TROLLEYS (l.c.)	$1–$3
TRUCKS (e.c.)	$3–$10
Real photo	$5–$35
TRUCKS (m.c.)	$3–$10
TRUCKS (l.c.)	$1–$3
p/TUCK (pmc), U.S. views	$10–$20
p/TUCK, Oilette, U.S. views	$3–$10
p/TUCK, other U.S. views	$3–$8
WATERMILLS (e.c.)	$1–$3
Real photo	$3–$10
WATERMILLS (m.c.)	$1–$2
WATERMILLS (l.c.)	$1–$2
WINDMILLS (e.c.)	$2–$5
Real photo	$3–$10
WINDMILLS (m.c.)	$1–$3
WINDMILLS (l.c.)	$1–$2
ZOOS (e.c.)	$1–$3
Real photo	$2–$5
ZOOS (m.c.)	$1–$2
ZOOS (l.c.)	$1–$2

Greeting Cards

Postcards with a greetings theme include many of the most desirable, as well as least desirable, designs. Most greeting cards with collector appeal mark specific holidays. But postcards were also produced with greetings not linked to any particular holiday. Most holiday greetings of collectible quality date from before World War I; some were also produced in the 1920s. Even today, as modern postcards flourish, there are few newly produced holiday greetings.

Postcard collectors have partly filled this void by creating their own postcard greetings, especially for National Postcard Week. This annual celebration-through-the-mail takes place during the first full week of May. (See the "Topical Cards" subsection titled "Postcard-Related" for examples.)

Most of the vast quantities of postcard greetings mailed by Americans before World War I have quite unremarkable designs. The surviving masses of such dull postcards comprise the "junk card" category available from dealers for 1 to 25 cents each or even by the pound! Postcard dealers seldom purchase such cards for re-sale unless they are acquired as part of an entire collection.

Junk greetings, however, are not worthless throwaways. They have little appeal to postcard collectors seeking quality images, but they have other uses. Junk greetings are frequently displayed in historic and product exhibits to enhance their nostalgic feel. Also, their address sides are scrutinized for value by philatelists, postal historians, and autograph collectors.

Ground-hog Day and Labor Day greetings received the least attention from postcard manufacturers. The surviving postcards are avidly sought. Rare Santa Claus designs, particularly Uncle Sam Santas and novelty Santas, are also widely sought.

Of major categories, Halloween postcards and Santa cards are the most widely collected. Jewish New Year greetings also have strong collector demand. Easter and Thanksgiving greetings have the least appeal to collectors at present.

The majority of illustrations in this section are pre–World War I greetings. The listings represent only greeting cards that collectors find "desirable." The value ranges reflect varying degrees of desirability (and topic).

Desirability depends on the quality of the illustration and design. Admittedly, this is a subjective aesthetic determination which each dealer, collector, buyer, and seller makes individually. Examples of unremarkable and desirable greetings drawn by Ellen H. Clapsaddle are shown on the following pages. Examples of highly desirable and aesthetically appealing designs are reproduced in color in the insert.

The holidays are listed in sequential order from the beginning to the end of the year. The emphasis is on American holidays.

GREETING CARD VALUES

New Year's Greetings: Coins, clovers, wishbones, swastikas, and pigs—all "good luck" symbols—are common on New Year's designs. Father Time, Little Time, and year-dates are frequent images.

NEW YEAR'S GREETINGS (pio.)	$30–$200
NEW YEAR'S GREETINGS (e.c.)	$1–$50
Artist-signed	$5–$30
Calendars	$3–$15
Children	$3–$15

Remember! All prices in this guide represent postcards in *Excellent* condition.

| Clover | $1–$5 |
| Coins | $3–$20 |

From the author's collection

A New Year's greeting with coins, pigs, and clover, all good luck symbols often found on New Year's greetings. This design is embossed with gold stamping over the coins; glitter outlines the four-leaf clovers. Printed in Europe. Divided back, ca. 1910. Not common. Value: $15.

Hold-to-lights	$10–$40
Pigs	$5–$30
Swastikas	$1–$10
Year-Dates (pre–1901)	$30–$50
Year-Dates (1901–1903)	$18–$20
Year-Dates (1904–1906)	$12–$15
Year-Dates (1907–1908)	$8–$10
Year-Dates (1909–1913)	$5–$8
Year-Dates (after 1913)	$8–$10

From the author's collection

A New Year's "year-date" greeting. The pigs' leis shape the new year "1909." A fantasy, "dressed pigs" (acting like humans) design, and a hold-to-light novelty. The design is also found as a plain year-date with no die-cut hold-to-light pattern. Scarce. Value: hold-to-light, $30; year-date, $12.

NEW YEAR'S GREETING (m.c., artist-signed)

$1–$20

Courtesy of John and Sandy Millns

Artist-signed Swedish New Year's greeting by Aina Stenberg. Published by Eskilholm, Sweden. Not common in the United States. Value: $12.

NEW YEAR'S GREETING (l.c.)	$1–$5
GROUND-HOG DAY (e.c.)	$150
GROUND-HOG DAY (m.c.)	$25

Courtesy of Postcard Collector

A very rare Ground-hog Day holiday greeting. One of a set of four different designs, one of several sets printed for this holiday. Value: $150.

LINCOLN'S BIRTHDAY (e.c.) $3–$15
    p/Anglo American: Open Book ser 726
                                        $20–$25
    p/Anglo American: Open Book ser 727
                                        $18–$20
    p/Bien $8–$10
    Blacks $5–$15
    Civil War scenes $3–$10
    p/International Art, s/Chapman $8–$10
    p/Lounsbury $10–$12
    p/Nash, ser 2, woman and torn flag
                                        $10–$12
    p/Nash, "Lincoln Centennial Souvenir"
                                        $8–$10

Courtesy of Joel Edler

A Lincoln's Birthday greeting. Copyright 1908 by E. Nash, Lincoln's Birthday Series 1, published for the 1909 centennial of Abraham Lincoln's birth. Embossed, gilding highlights. Common. Value: $6.

    p/PFB, ser 9463, 9464 $12–$15
    p/Sander, ser 415 $8–$10
    p/Sheahan $8–$10
    p/Taggert, ser 606 $8–$10
    p/Tuck, ser 155 (6 des) $10–$12
    p/Wolf, s/Ferris $8–$10

Remember! All prices in this guide represent postcards in *Excellent* condition.

Valentine's Greetings: Sentimental messages and images of hearts, flowers, and cupids fill most Valentine greetings. Better designs show children and beautiful women, are artist-signed, or have novel treatments such as silk, embossing, or gilding.

The John Winsch, Schmucker-style beautiful woman printed on silk on cards with embossed and gilded border designs are among the most beautiful of American antique postcards.

Vinegar Valentines—postcards with comical insults—are desirable for their social content.

VALENTINE'S GREETINGS (e.c.)	$1–$150
s/Clapsaddle	$5–$15
s/Clapsaddle: votes for women, women's work	$35–$100
Comic Valentines	$3–$5
s/EHD	$4–$8

Courtesy of Joel Edler

Pre–World War I embossed card with gilding highlights. Artist-signed EHD (Ethel Dewees), published by aMp Co. The "cupid" kid and the fire-fighting theme add topical interest. Common. Value: $6.

The minimum value in this price guide is $1. While many dealers offer 25-cent and 50-cent "bargain boxes," few dealers sort, individually price, and protectively "sleeve" postcards valued at less than $1. This price guide offers values for postcards worth $1 or more.

s/Heinmuller $8–$12

A monk-child with cupid wings on a divided-back sentimental greeting, #1512, from International Art publishers. Artist-signed Heinmuller. Not common. Value: $8.

p/International Art, ser 15810, pinwheel
                                      $35–$40
s/J. Johnson $6–$10

A soldier boy-child and two little girls on a neatly designed and bordered card, artist-signed J. Johnson. Published by Gabriel, Valentine Series 407. Not common. Value: $8.

p/Langsdorf $4–$8
p/MAB, silk appliqué $15–$20
s/MEP $8–$12
p/Nash $4–$6

| p/Nister | $4–$6 |
| p/PFB | $6–$10 |

Courtesy of Joel Edler

A precious moment between child and dog. Embossed design, gilding highlights, printed by Stecher Litho Co. of Rochester, New York, series 517E. Artist-signed MEP (Margaret Evans Price). Not common. Value: $8.

Courtesy of Fred Schiffman

Valentine kitsch: cute cupids, flower garlands, and a large heart. Common. Value: $3.

p/Rotograph	$6–$10
p/Stecher	$4–$6
p /Tuck	$6–$8
Vinegar Valentines	$4–$10

p/Winsch $3–$100

Courtesy of Joel Edler

*The Schmucker-style beautiful woman design is printed on silk.
The hearts and outlines of the border design are overlaid with
gold. Printed in Germany, published by John Winsch. Rare.* Value:
$80.

From the author's collection

*Valentine glamour: a Schmucker-style beautiful woman. Pub-
lished by John Winsch. Scarce.* Value: $35.

p/Wolf, s/Clapsaddle	$6–$10
VALENTINE'S GREETINGS (m.c.)	$2–$10
Vinegar Valentines	$3–$8
p/Whitney	$3–$8
VALENTINE'S GREETINGS (l.c.)	$1–$2
WASHINGTON'S BIRTHDAY (e.c.)	$3–$15
p/Anglo American, Open Book ser 725	
	$10–$15

p/Anglo American, Open Book ser 728

$12–$15

p/Bien, ser 760 $4–$6

s/Clapsaddle $8–$12

Courtesy of Joel Edler

A cute child and a flag-draped portrait of Washington form the design for this Washington's Birthday greeting. Artist-signed Ellen H. Clapsaddle, #16250, published by International Art, printed in Germany, embossed with gilding highlights. Common. Value: $10.

p/GDD, ser 2161	$5–$6
p/International Art	$5–$12
p/L & E, s/H. B. Griggs	$6–$12
p/Nash	$5–$12
p/Sander, ser 414	$5–$6
p/Taggert, ser 605	$4–$5

The minimum value in this price guide is $1. While many dealers offer 25-cent and 50-cent "bargain boxes," few dealers sort, individually price, and protectively "sleeve" postcards valued at less than $1. This price guide offers values for postcards worth $1 or more.

p/Tuck $5–$10

Washington's Birthday Series 178, published by Raphael Tuck.
Divided-back card, cancelled in 1913. Common. Value: $8.

LEAP YEAR GREETINGS (e.c.)	$5–$15
s/Brill (1912)	$6–$8
p/Gabriel, s/DWIG, ser 401	$8–$10

A 1908 Leap Year greeting, artist-signed DWIG. Copyright Samuel
Gabriel Sons & Co., New York. Not common. Value: $8.

p/Sander, s/Hutaf, ser 217	$8–$10
p/Tuck, s/Lance Thackery	$8–$10
ST. PATRICK'S DAY GREETINGS (e.c.)	$2–$60
Children	$5–$15

s/Clapsaddle $5–$15

Courtesy of Joel Edler

A pre–World War I (postally used in 1916) divided-back card, artist-signed Ellen H. Clapsaddle. One of a beautiful group of embossed St. Patrick's Day designs by International Art. A mirror image of this design was published by Wolf. Scarce. Value: $15.

s/Gene Carr $6–$10

Courtesy of Fred Schiffman

The Day the Dutch lead the Irish.

A comic St. Patrick's Day greeting with an ethnic insult, artist-signed Gene Carr. An undivided-back card, copyright 1906 by the Rotograph Co., New York, #FL191. Not common. Value: $10.

Ethnic slurs	$3–$15
Pipes	$2–$3
Shillelagh	$3–$10

s/SLS (Schmucker) $20–$60

From the author's collection

The center design of a young woman riding an Irish pipe is printed on silk. The card's border is embossed; the St. Patrick's greeting and the clovers are overlaid with gold. The initials SLS (of artist Samuel L. Schmucker) appear in the upper left area of the inner design. Rare. Value: $60.

p/Tuck $3–$10

Courtesy of Fred Schiffman

A St. Patrick's Day greeting with a song theme. From Raphael Tuck's postcard series 157, "The Emerald Isle." Common. Value: $6.

p/Winsch	$3–$60
ST. PATRICK'S DAY GREETINGS (m.c.)	$1–$5
ST. PATRICK'S DAY GREETINGS (l.c.)	$1–$2
APRIL FOOL'S DAY GREETINGS (e.c.)	$2–$25
p//(in France)	$8–$150
p/Koeber, s/Hutaf	$10–$15
p/Ullman, s/Wall	$15–$20

EASTER GREETINGS (e.c.)	$2–$30
Angels	$2–$6
Artist-signed	$5–$30

Courtesy of John and Sandy Millns

A Swedish Easter greeting, artist-signed Jenny Nystrom, the most prolific Swedish postcard artist as well as the Swedish postcard artist most commonly seen by American Collectors. A cute child in a field of flowers is the subject. Not common. Value: $15.

| Bunnies | $2–$15 |

Courtesy of Fred Schiffman

A bunny playing diabolo, a ball and string game seen on a number of postcard designs avidly sought by some collectors; #E-37, copyright by Nash. Value: $8.

| Chicks | $2–$15 |

Children $5–$15

Courtesy of Fred Schiffman

A cute Easter greeting design of a role reversal—the bunny is discovering the girl in the basket! Artist-signed Katharine Gassaway, published by Raphael Tuck & Sons, Easter Post Cards Series 130. Not common. Value: $10.

Easter witches (Swedish)	$10–$25
Eggs	$2–$5
Hold-to-light	$25 –$40
Novelty	$10–$30

From the author's collection

A dressed chick and bunny and a novelty pinwheel egg make a first-rate Easter postcard! This is #404704, printed in Europe. The phrase "Depose DRGM," seen at the bottom of this design, is often mistakenly confused for the publisher's name. The phrase actually means: Deutsches Reichsgemuster, a registered design! A scarce card. Value: $35.

p/PFB $5–$25

Courtesy of Joel Edler

*Beautifully designed, printed, embossed, and gilded, this post-
card of an Easter lamb hitched to an Easter egg is a fine example
of a quality PFB postcard; #5837, postally used in 1909. Not
common. Value: $20.*

EASTER GREETINGS (m.c.)	$2–$10
EASTER GREETINGS (l.c.)	$1–$2
MEMORIAL (DECORATION) DAY GREETINGS (e.c.)	
	$2–$20
Battlegrounds	$2–$5
Cemeteries	$2–$5
Confederate memorial	$5–$10
Flags and bunting	$2–$5
p/Gabriel, ser 150	$12–$15
p/International Art, s/Chapman	$8–$10
p/International Art, s/Clapsaddle	
	$3–$10
p/Lounsbury, s/Bunnell	$10–$12
p/Nash, ser 1–5	$6–$10
p/Nash, ser 6	$12–$15
p/Tuck, Decoration Day ser 107	$8–$10
p/Tuck, Decoration Day ser 158	$10–$12
p/Tuck, Decoration Day ser 173	$15–$18
p/Tuck, Decoration Day ser 179	$12–$15
p/Tuck, Memorial (Confederate) Day	
	$15–$18
FOURTH OF JULY GREETINGS (e.c.)	$5–$50
p/Bien, ser 700, 705, 710	$6–$10
p/Bien, ser 715	$10–$12
Children	$5–$15

s/Clapsaddle	$5–$15
Firecrackers	$5–$8
p/GDD, ser 2099	$8–$10
p/GDD, ser 2172	$10–$12
p/International Art, s/Clapsaddle	
	$5–$15
p/International Art, s/Chapman	
	$10–$12
p/Lounsbury	$10–$12
p/Lounsbury, ser 2076, s/Bunnell	
	$10–$12
p/MAB (airbrush)	$8–$10
p/Nash, ser 1–6	$6–$10
p/Nash, ser 7	$4–$6
p/Nash, ser 8	$10–$12

Courtesy of Fred Schiffman

Cute kids, a dog, firecrackers, and flags: an embossed, gilded design, published by Nash. Not common. Value: $10.

p/PFB, ser 8252	$12–$15
p/PFB, ser 9507, s/Bunnell	$15–$40
p/Sander	$8–$10

The minimum value in this price guide is $1. While many dealers offer 25-cent and 50-cent "bargain boxes," few dealers sort, individually price, and protectively "sleeve" postcards valued at less than $1. This price guide offers values for postcards worth $1 or more.

p/Tuck, ser 109	*$8–$10*
p/Tuck, ser 159	*$10–$12*
p/Ullman, s/Wall	*$10–$12*
LABOR DAY GREETINGS (e.c.)	*$100–$200*
p/Lounsbury, ser 2046 (4 des)	*$200*
p/Nash, ser 1 (2 des)	*$150*
JEWISH NEW YEAR (e.c.)	*$5–$50*

From the author's collection

Jewish New Year postcard greeting printed in a plain box bordered by fabric design. A Wiener Werkstätte publication. Not common. Value: $35.

Halloween Greetings have been so popular that prices may be double that of a similar design for another holiday. Demand has leveled off, but prices have remained firm.

The most desirable of Halloween greetings are the designs copyrighted by John Winsch. Many are attributed to the American artist Samuel L. Schmucker and others to Jason Freixas. A checklist of Winsch Halloween designs compiled by Hazel E. Lelar is a valuable aid to serious collectors of this material.

HALLOWEEN GREETINGS (e.c.)	*$5–$150*
p/Anglo American, ser 876	*$12–$15*
p/Auburn	*$8–$10*
p/Austen	*$8–$10*
p/BW, ser 374	*$12–$15*

s/E. C. Banks $12–$15

Courtesy of Joel Edler

An attractive young woman bobbing for apples adds a glamour theme to this Halloween greeting. Jack-o'-lantern-bordered, artist-signed E. C. Banks, embossed, printed in Germany. Postally used in 1909. Not common. Value: $12.

p/Bergman $8–$15
p/Bien, ser 980 $12–$15
s/Frances Brundage $10–$15

Courtesy of Fred Schiffman

Four girls in party dresses and ribbons dance around a smiling jack-o'-lantern. Artist-signed and Frances Brundage copyright, printed with a wide embossed red border, published by Gabriel. Not common. Value: $15.

s/Clapsaddle $5–$15
s/Clapsaddle, p/Wolf, ser 501 $15–$40
s/Clapsaddle, mechanical, ser 1236
                                  $150–$200
p/Davis $10–$12
p/Detroit $20–$30

s/DWIG $25–$30

Courtesy of Fred Schiffman

One of a series of six glamorous Halloween witches, unsigned DWIG, series 981, published by J. Marks. Scarce. Value: $25.

p/Fairman $5–$10
s/Freixas $30–$50

Courtesy of John and Sandy Milins

Delicately drawn child, jack-o'-lantern, and kitten. Copyright 1914 by John Winsch. The artwork is attributed to Jason Freixas. A scarce card. Value: $50.

Remember! All prices in this guide represent postcards in *Excellent* condition.

p/Gabriel $10–$15

Courtesy of Joel Edler

A Halloween witch with black cat on her broomstick. Artist-signed Frances Brundage, published by Gabriel, Halloween Series 120. Postally used 1911. Common. Value: $12.

p/Garre, s/Clapsaddle	$8–$10
p/Gartner & Bender	$4–$10
p/Gibson Art	$5–$10
p/Gottshalk, Dreyfuss & Davis	$6–$12
s/H. B. Griggs	$5–$15
p/International Art, s/Clapsaddle	
	$10–$15
p/International Art, ser 1236, mechanical	
	$150–$200
p/International Art, s/Wall	$12–$15
p/Langsdorf	$8–$12
p/L & E, s/H. B. Griggs	$8–$15
p/Lounsbury, ser 2052	$12–$15
p/Marks, ser 981	$25–$30

The minimum value in this price guide is $1. While many dealers offer 25-cent and 50-cent "bargain boxes," few dealers sort, individually price, and protectively "sleeve" postcards valued at less than $1. This price guide offers values for postcards worth $1 or more.

p/Nash $10–$25

*A pretty maid protects herself with a ring of pumpkin seeds to
ward away the witches, goblins, and other Halloween creatures.
Postally used 1914, embossed, copyright E. Nash, #H-12. Not
common. Value: $15.*

p/Owen	$6–$12
p/PFB, ser 9422	$10–$20
p/Robbins	$6–$10
p/Rose	$8–$15
p/Samson Bros.	$12–$15

*A black cat drives a jack-o'-lantern carriage pulled by six mice!
The Halloween greeting is gilded, embossed, and bordered with a
colorful checkered design. Postally used in 1912, the card is
#S500, attributed to Samson Bros. Not common. Value: $15.*

p/Sander	$12–$15
p/Santway, ser 140	$10–$15

p/Stecher $10–$15

From the author's collection

One of six striking black, yellow, and orange designs of a child and jack-o'-lantern. Stecher series 57B, copyright JEP (James E. Pitts). Not common. Value: $15.

p/Stern $8–$15
p/TP & Co. $8–$12
p/Taggert, ser 803, 804 $10–$12
p/Tuck $10–$15

Courtesy of Joel Edler

A loving witch and her black cat sit on a pumpkin. Published by Raphael Tuck, Halloween Series 174, an unsigned Brundage design. Not common. Value: $15.

p/Tuck, ser 807, unsigned Wiederseim
$20–$30
p/Tuck, ser 100, unsigned Schmucker
$30–$35
p/Ullman, s/Wall $12–$15
p/Valentine $8–$12
p/Volland $5–$10
s/Wall $12–$15
p/Winsch $50–$120

Courtesy of Postcard Collector

A glamour theme on a Halloween greeting. The design is copyright 1911 by John Winsch. The Winsch designs are among the most widely desired of Halloween cards. Scarce. Value: $75.

Courtesy of *Postcard Collector*

A John Winsch Halloween design with a yellow and black border. A rare postcard. Value: $50–$75.

Courtesy of Joel Edler

A John Winsch design, copyright 1912. A highly desirable Halloween postcard. Value: $75.

Courtesy of Joel Edler

A John Winsch Halloween design, copyright 1911. A beautiful sleeping maiden is protected by good fairies as hordes of goblins hover in the background. A full moon shines in the window. Attributed to Samuel L. Schmucker, as are many other Winsch Halloweens. Scarce. Value: $75.

p/Wolf, ser 501, s/Clapsaddle	$20–$40
p/Whitney	$5–$15
HALLOWEEN GREETINGS (m.c.)	$3–$10
p/Metropolitan	$3–$10
HALLOWEEN GREETINGS (l.c.)	$1–$5
p/Hallmark	$1–$5

THANKSGIVING GREETINGS (e.c.)	$1–$75
Children	$3–$10
Comic	$1–$10
Feasts	$1–$10
s/H. B. Griggs, p/ L & E	$3–$15

Courtesy of Joel Edler

Artist-signed HBG (H. B. Griggs), the girl is preparing Thanksgiving pies for her dollies, one of which is black. L & E series 2263, embossed, published by Leubrie & Elkus. Not common. Value: $15.

Mechanical $40–$50

From the author's collection

A pinwheel mechanical of two Thanksgiving turkeys, one of six different designs. Published by Arthur Strofer. Pre–World War I, scarce. Value: $40.

p/Sander	$4–$6
p/Tuck	$4–$8
Turkeys	$1–$3
Uncle Sam	$10–$20
s/Veenfliet	$6–$8
p/Winsch	$15–$30

p/Winsch (projection) $60–$75

Courtesy of Joel Edler

A John Winsch design, copyright 1911, printed in Germany, postally used 1912. An attractive maiden and turkey. An embossed
postcard. Value: $25.The identical design is also found on a nov-
elty "projection" postcard—the maiden, printed on separate stock,
projects forward from the underlying card. Value: $75.

THANKSGIVING GREETINGS (m.c.)	$1–$5
THANKSGIVING GREETINGS (l.c.)	$1–$3
HANUKKAH GREETINGS (e.c.)	$5–$50
HANUKKAH GREETINGS (m.c.)	$2–$20
HANUKKAH GREETINGS (l.c.)	$1–$10

Courtesy of Nu-Vista Prints

A current-issue view card of the Cleveland, Ohio, skyline with a
menorah and Hanukkah greeting overlay. Published in 1989 by
Nu-Vista Prints. Value: $25–$50

Christmas and Santas: Collectors find a wide variety of desirable designs among Christmas, and especially Santa, postcards. There is a broad range of subject matter, from artist-signed and advertising, to rare mechanicals, silks, hold-to-lights, and other novelties. There is good supply and demand for desirable postcards of most subject matter in most price ranges. Die-cut, hold-to-light, Uncle Sam Santas are an exception, where potential buyers far outnumber known supply.

Christmas greetings without a Santa image are listed first. Santas follow, under "Christmas Santa Greetings."

CHRISTMAS GREETINGS (pio.)	$50–$200
CHRISTMAS GREETINGS (e.c.)	$1–$100
Advertising	$5–$100
Angels	$3–$10
Artist-signed	$5–$100
Children	$5–$25

Courtesy of Fred Schiffman

Four children anticipate the flavor as their mother brings out a Christmas pudding. Artist-signed HBG (H. B. Griggs), this greeting portrays blacks in a positive light. Series 2224, published by Leubrie & Elkus. Not common. Value: $20.

s/Clapsaddle	$8–$25
Dolls and toys	$5–$50
Hold-to-light, die-cut	$30–$75
Hold-to-light, transparency	$15–$40
Holly-floral	$1–$5
p/Illustrated Postal Card	$2–$10
p/International Art	$3–$20
p/Langsdorf	$2–$10
p/Nash	$1–$10

p/Nister	$5–$20
p/PFB	$5–$20
Real photo	$5–$20

Courtesy of Joel Edler

Real photo postcard of a girl with her Christmas presents—teddy bear, toys, and books—under the Christmas tree. In front of the girl is an open postcard album. Value: $20.

Snowmen	$3–$20
p/Stecher	$3–$15
p/Winsch	$8–$35

From the author's collection

Outdoor winter scene of two pretty girls in their winter coats. Copyright 1912 by publisher John Winsch. Embossed, gilding. Not common. Value: $15.

p/Wolf	$1–$10
CHRISTMAS GREETINGS (m.c.)	$1–$20
p/Whitney	$3–$12
CHRISTMAS GREETINGS (l.c.)	$1–$10

CHRISTMAS SANTA GREETINGS (pio.) $20–$200
CHRISTMAS SANTA GREETINGS (e.c.) $2–$1000

Courtesy of Fred Schiffman

*Santa kitsch. An ordinary and unremarkable Santa postcard de-
sign. A common postcard. Even though it's 80 years old and the
subject is Santa, it has a low value.* Value: $3.

Advertising $10–$250

Courtesy of Joel Edler

*Santa Claus used in a bank promotion. One of a series of twelve
calendar postcards for 1912. Rare.* Value: $30.

Remember! All prices in this guide represent postcards in
Excellent condition.

Courtesy of Joel Edler

Santa Claus delivering Falstaff beer. A very rare advertising post-card for Falstaff beer incorporates a 20-year calendar. A quality design on a card filled with "collectible" topics: advertising, beer, Santa, Christmas greeting, mechanical, calendar! Value: $150.

Artist-signed $10–$150

Courtesy of John and Sandy Millns

Artist-signed Kathryn Elliott card combines a glamour theme with Santa Claus on a Christmas greeting. Not common. Value: $10.

    w/Autos $10–$100
    p/BW $8–$15

Children $3–$20

Courtesy of Joel Edler

A MERRY CHRISTMAS
SOMETIMES I HAVE TROUBLE
GETTING DOWN THE CHIMNEY
BECAUSE I'M SO FAT, BUT I
MANAGED TO FILL YOUR STOCKINGS

A child Santa is the theme on this Charles Twelvetrees artist-signed Christmas greeting. Pre–World War I, #1034. Common. Value: $5.

p/Davidson Bros.	$5–$15
p/EAS	$5–$15
Embroidered	$15–$25

From the author's collection

A Merry Christmas

An embroidered Santa Claus Christmas greeting. Embroidered postcards were frequently brought back from Europe by soldiers in World War I. Not common. Value: $20.

Glamour   *$10–$40*

*"Miss Santa Claus," artist-signed Harrison Fisher, #182. Pub-
lished by Reinthal & Newman. Not common.* Value: $10.

Hold-to-light, die-cut   *$100–$1,000*
Hold-to-light, transparency   *$50–$100*

*Left. Two girls lean out the window to reach the toys in Santa's
bag. This Santa image appears in a variety of formats on Christmas postcards: as a flat-printed card, embossed, with metallic
gilding outlining the image, with a glaze surface, as a "squeaker,"
as die-cut and transparency hold-to-lights, with velvet appliqué,
and possibly in other formats too. Ca. 1909. Scarce to rare.* Value:
flat, $10; embossed, gilded or glaze, $15; appliqué, $20; transpar-
ency hold-to-light, $60; die-cut hold-to-light, $100; squeaker, $150.
*Right. Transparency hold-to-light Santa. The same image as pre-
vious figure except that the concealed Santa only appears when
the card is held up to a bright light. The Santa image is printed on
an inner layer of paper.*

Installment (set of 4) $200

Santa Claus on a four-card installment series published by Franz Huld of New York in 1906. This is one of the more desirable of the fourteen installment series Huld published. Rare. Value: $250.

Krampus $25–$50

Courtesy of John and Sandy Millins

Will you have a spin with me tonight.

Krampus—the devil Santa—playing diabolo. B & R Series. Not common. Value: $35.

p/L & E	$10–$20
p/Langsdorf	$10–$20
Leather	$8–$20
p/MAB	$8–$15
p/Marks	$8–$15
Mechanical	$50–$250

Courtesy of Joel Edler

Guillotine-style mechanical. As the tab is pushed up, the image in the window changes from a boy to a pipe-smoking Santa Claus wearing a green suit and carrying a sack. Printed in Germany, ca. 1909. The Santa and boy design is also found in other postcard formats including a die-cut hold-to-light. Very rare. Value: mechanical, $250; die-cut hold-to-light, $150.

Courtesy of Joel Edler

The *"glass window"* behind Santa is really three layers of white-spotted celluloid. When the layers of celluloid are moved in different directions, it appears that snow is falling. This blue-suited Santa image also occurs on a die-cut hold-to-light. Printed in Germany, ca. 1909. Very rare. Value: mechanical, $250; die-cut hold-to-light, $150.

p/Nash	$3–$15
p/PFB	$15–$25
Real hair	$80–$100
Real photo	$8–$25
p/Rotograph	$5–$20
p/Samson Bros.	$3–$15
Silk appliqué	$40–$50
Squeakers	$100
w/Toys	$5–$30
p/Tuck	$8–$30

The minimum value in this price guide is $1. While many dealers offer 25-cent and 50-cent "bargain boxes," few dealers sort, individually price, and protectively "sleeve" postcards valued at less than $1. This price guide offers values for postcards worth $1 or more.

Uncle Sam $250–$1,000

Courtesy of Joel Edler

*The ultimate in Santa Claus Christmas greetings is the Uncle Sam
Santa Claus. These highly desirable greetings are very rare. Four
different images are known; they were reproduced on the covers
of the December 1984, 1985, 1986, and 1987 issues of* Postcard
Collector *magazine. The images have been seen in embossed
and also die-cut hold-to-light formats. Few copies of these
postcards are known to exist and only estimated values can be
offered. Estimated Value: embossed, $250–$300; die-cut hold-to-
light, $1,000+.*

p/United Art	$3–$15
P/Volland	$2–$15
CHRISTMAS SANTA GREETINGS (m.c.)	$1–$75
Advertising	$5–$75

Courtesy of Joel Edler

*Santa Claus on a Christmas advertising card for Wolverine Speed-
ster wagons, scooters, and bikes. Artist-signed Deady. Mailed
from the Cable Hardware Co. in Lansing, Michigan, on December 6, 1923, to Josephine Joy of Nelsonville, Ohio. Value: $60.*

Courtesy of Joel Edler

Santa on an advertising postcard urges men to "Dress up for Xmas" with Clinton's fine clothes; #E-10938 published by E. B. Thomas of Cambridge, Massachusetts, 1940s(?). Not common. Value: $20.

Artist-signed $3–$30

Courtesy of John and Sandy Millns

Artist-signed F. G. Lewin. On this Christmas greeting the children have captured Santa and he is imprisoned in a wagon pulled by one reindeer wearing lanterns on its antlers. A golliwog doll is stuffed in the stocking hanging from the rail. This is # 2299 published by J. Salmon Sevenoaks. Late 1920s. Value: $30.

p/Whitney	$2–$20
CHRISTMAS SANTA GREETINGS (l.c.)	$1–$10
BIRTHDAY GREETINGS (e.c.)	$1–$20
Novelty	$2–$20
BIRTHDAY GREETINGS (m.c.)	$1–$5
BIRTHDAY GREETINGS (l.c.)	$1–$3

Artist-Signed Cards

An artist-signed postcard is one where the artist's signature is included within the artwork as it is reproduced on the card. It should not be confused with an actual autograph added after the postcard is printed. An autograph will add a significant premium to the value of a postcard for someone well known but may add little value for someone unknown.

Most artist-signed postcards were produced during the early part of this century. Thousands of illustrators created work that was reproduced on postcards. Much of the work cannot be attributed to a specific artist. Only a fraction of identifiable work actually bears the artist's signature on the art itself. Of this group, a relatively small number of artists are avidly collected for the artwork rather than for the subject.

A large proportion of collectible artist-signed postcards falls within the groupings of glamour, children, and humor. In other subject areas the artist-signed postcard may be valued at a slight premium over the desirability of the subject itself.

Artist-signed postcards originally produced for European consumption find an avid audience in the United States. (This is in sharp contrast to the relatively low popularity of non-U.S. views, topicals, and greetings. Indeed, an identical holiday design bearing the phrase "Frohliche Weihnachten" or "Joyeux Noelle" may be passed over for one with a "Merry Christmas" greeting, even though the foreign postcard is priced lower!) Of particular interest, and bearing high values, are the early-century Art Nouveau and Art Deco artist-signed glamour postcards from many European countries.

The listings that follow cover artist-drawn postcards. Examples of photographer-signed postcards are found in the "View Cards" section. These listings are not comprehensive, but rather concentrate on the postcards of collected artists. Representative work is illustrated for many major artists. Artist-signed cards are also illustrated under appropriate subjects in the "View Cards," "Greeting Cards," and "Topical Cards" sections of this price guide.

Some early artist-signed postcards are reproductions of work originally published as posters, magazine illustrations, or pictures for framing, just as some contemporary artist-signed postcards are reproductions of earlier postcards. Whenever possible, specific publishers are listed rather than stating that the postcard is an original or a reproduction.

The entries are listed alphabetically by the artist's last name. When an artist's initials commonly appear on the postcard, they are listed alphabetically by first initial and referenced to the full-name entry, when known.

ARTIST-SIGNED CARD VALUES

ANGELL, CLARE **(British)** $5–$15

Courtesy of Fred Schiffman

Signed Clare Angell, published by the prolific British publisher Bamforth. A kicking goat, the ship's mascot ("John Bull"), has no use for visiting "Willie-Boys." The postcard was probably published and the humor probably relates to the period when William Howard Taft was president, 1909–1913. Not common. Value: $8.

ARMSTRONG, ROLF (American) $15–$25

Courtesy of John and Sandy Milins

Signed Rolf Armstrong. The postcard is copyright Knapp Co., New York, and probably dates from after World War I. A beautiful young woman is the subject; the card would be classified in the "American Girl" or glamour category. Not common. Value: $20.

ASTI, ANGELO (French, 1847–1903) $5–$35
p/Tuck $10–$35

Courtesy of John and Sandy Milins

Signed A. Asti. This pre–World War I postcard design of a beautiful woman by Angelo Asti was published by H. G. Zimmerman of Chicago. Not common. Value: $10.

ATWELL, MABEL LUCIE (English, 1879–1964)

$5–$30

"I SHOULD FINK THAT STORKS ABOUT AGAIN!"

Signed Mabel Lucie Atwell. This English artist produced postcard designs of delightful plump-cheeked, pudgy-legged children for Raphael Tuck & Sons and Valentine & Sons from the teens to the 1940s. This example dates from the late teens. Not common. Value: $8.

BANKS, E. C. $10–$20

BARBER, COURT $5–$20

Signed Court Barber '13, card #668, published by RHB. A delicate postcard design in the glamour category. Not common. Value: $8.

Signed Court Barber '13, card #690, published by RHB. Outdoor winter scenes occur far less frequently in the glamour category than the portrait vignettes, but the low level of interest for them has kept prices steady. Not common. Value: $8.

BERTIGLIA, A. **(Italian)**   *$8–$20*

Signed A. Bertiglia. Children playing soldier. Published by CCM. Not common. Value: $12.

BIRGER **(Swedish)**   **$5–$15**

Courtesy of John and Sandy Millns

GOTT NYTT ÅR.

Signed Birger. Swedish New Year's greeting. Divided-back card, probably 1940s. Not common. Value: $10.

BISHOP, C. **(American)**   **$3–$15**

From the author's collection

Signed Bishop. Popular American humorist whose subjects ranged from courtship and marriage to ethnic stereotypes and professions. The scissors grinder is one in a series that also includes a waffle man and an ice vendor. Note the Buster Brown-like character. Not common. Value: $8.

BLODGETT, BERTHA $3–$10
   Signed art $6–$10
   Unsigned art $3–$5
BOILEAU, PHILIP (Canadian-American, 1864–1917)
                                             $15–$45
p/Metropolitan Insurance calendar ads
                                             $35–$45
p/Reinthal & Newman $15–$25
Series 109 $20–$30
p/Tuck $75–$100

Courtesy of Joel Edler

Signed Philip Boileau. "Winter Whispers . . .," copyright 1907 and published by Reinthal & Newman, was postally used in 1910. This dreamy-eyed model conveyed the idealized beauty of the American female. Not common. Value: $18.

From the author's collection

Signed Philip Boileau. "I Don't Care!" Published by Reinthal & Newman. Not common. Value: $18.

BOMPARD, S. (Italian) $5–$20

Courtesy of John and Sandy Millns

Signed S. Bompard. Card #459–11, divided back, probably 1920s. Italian glamour. Not common. Value: $15.

BREGER, DAVID (American, 1908–1970) $5–$15
BRETT, MOLLY (English) $5–$20
     Nursery rhymes p/Medici Society $5–$10
BRILL, GEORGE REITER (1867–1918), "Ginks"

                               $6–$10
BROWN, KEN (American) $1–$5

From the author's collection

BEWARE OF GEEKS BEARING GIFTS

Signed Ken Brown. American. Ken Brown captured the essence of 1980's American yuppiedom with well-focused humor. Common. Value: $2.

BROWNE, TOM (English, 1872–1910) $5–$20
     Advertising postcards $10–$20
     p/Davidson Bros. $5–$10
     Humor/social commentary $5–$20

BRUNDAGE, FRANCES (1854–1937)

	$5–$40
Halloween greetings, p/Gabriel	$10–$15
p/Tuck, undivided back	$30–$40
p/Tuck, "Colored Folks" Oilette	$15–$20
Greetings, divided back	$5–$20

Signed Frances Brundage. An undivided-back card, #674, "Evening Prayer" from the Mother's Darling Series published by Raphael Tuck. The blank area on the right half of the postcard design allowed the sender to write a message. Before 1907 in the United States (in Britain the change came years earlier), no message could be written on the address side of the postcard. Scarce. Value: $40.

BUNNELL, C. B. (American)	$5–$40
p/PFB, ser 9057, 4th July	$25–$40
BURD, CLARA M. (American)	$5–$30
Cradle Roll birthday greetings	$5–$10
Nursery rhymes, p/Fralinger's Taffy	
	$25–$30

Signed C. M. Burd. A first-birthday greeting. Not common. Value: $8.

CMR (*see* Charles M. Russell)

CARR, GENE (American, b. 1881)   *$6–$15*

    p/Rotograph, July 4th greetings *$10–$12*

    p/Rotograph, St. Patrick's greetings

                                    $8–$10

CAVALLY, FREDERICK L. (humor)   *$1–$10*

CHAPMAN, C. (American, patriotic)   *$5–$15*

CHERET (French)   *$80–$120*

Courtesy of John and Sandy Millns

Signed Cheret. An Art Nouveau-style illustration of a couple skating at the Ice Palace on the Champs Élysées. An undivided-back card, #10, published in Paris by Editions Cinos. Rare. Value: $120.

CHIOSTRI, CARLO (Italian, 1863–1939) *$30–$80*

CHIOSTRI, SOFIA (Italian)   *$20–$100*

CHRISTY, F. EARL (American)   *$5–$75*

Courtesy of John and Sandy Millns

Signed F. Earl Christy. This postcard in the College Girls Series, #2767 (College Queens), combines the themes of beautiful women, college hoopla, and playing cards. Cancelled in 1909. A desirable postcard. Scarce. Value: $70. (Most Christys fall in the $10–$15 range.)

CHRISTY, HOWARD CHANDLER (American) $5–$15
> Jamestown Expo, Navy girl and Army girl
> $75

CLAPSADDLE, ELLEN H. (American, 1865–1934)

	$1–$200
Christmas greetings	$5–$20
Easter greetings	$5–$10
Halloween greetings	$10–$40
Halloween mechanicals	$150–$200
Independence Day greetings	$5–$12
Lincoln's Birthday greetings	$5–$10
New Year's Day greetings	$5–$15
St. Patrick's Day greetings	$5–$12
Suffrage-related	$50–$100
Thanksgiving greetings	$1–$10
Valentine's greetings	$5–$10
Valentine's mechanicals	$20–$40
Washington's Birthday	$5–$10

From the author's collection

Signed Ellen H. Clapsaddle. The Valentine's greeting, the children theme, the artist's signature, and the woman's suffrage theme all contribute to the value of this postcard. More importantly, it is a variation of an earlier design published by International Art. The original design was embossed and is identical to, but a mirror image of, the postcard illustrated; its value is $50. This variant was published by Wolf & Co. of Philadelphia. Value: $100.

CLARK, ROSE $5–$20
CLAY, JOHN CECIL (American) $10–$30

Courtesy of Fred Schiffman

Signed John Cecil Clay. A finely printed simple, but subtle, illus-
tration of a woman's beautiful face combined with a flower and
nature theme; #FL166, published by the Rotograph Co., copyright
by the artist. Scarce. Value: $25.

COFFIN, HASKELL $10–$20

Courtesy of John and Sandy Millns

Signed Haskell Coffin, "The Lure of the Poppies." Copyright 1913
by R.C. Co., New York. Not common. Value: $15.

CORBETT, BERTHA (American, children) $5–$20
CRITE $5–$15

Courtesy of Fred Schiffman

*Signed Crite. Billy Possum (Taft) eats Teddy Bear (Roosevelt),
"Mountain House" style! This is the most desirable example in a
set that is difficult to complete. Copyright 1909 by L. Gulick.
Scarce.* Value: $12.

CURTIS, E. (Elizabeth), p/Tuck $5–$15
DANIELL, EVA (Glamour) $75–$150

Courtesy of John and Sandy Milins

*Signed Eva Daniell. A beautiful Art Nouveau design with intricate
detail work. The undivided-back card leaves space on the image
side for a message; #2525 in the Tuck Modern Art Series.
Rare.* Value: $150.

DAVIS, JIM (American, l.c., Garfield designs)

$1–$2

DESCH, FRANK (American) $15–$30

Courtesy of John and Sandy Millns

*Signed Frank Desch. "Lillian," #303, copyright by the Knapp Co.,
New York, published by Paul Heckscher. Not common. Value: $20.*

DEWEES, ETHEL (E.D.) $5–$20
DIXON, DOROTHY (children) $5–$20
DRAYTON (*see* Grace Wiederseim)
DRUMMOND, NORAH $5–$20

Courtesy of John and Sandy Millns

*Signed Drummond. "Man's Best Friend," a Tuck Oilette postcard,
#8650. Norah Drummond produced a large quantity of animal
postcard designs. Not common. Value: $10.*

DUNCAN, FREDERICK (American) $5–$20

Signed Frederick Duncan. "Reflecting," #136, copyright by the Knapp Co., New York. Not common. Value: $15.

DWIG (*see* Dwiggins)

DWIGGINS, CLARE VICTOR (American, 1874–1959)

	$5–$35
Halloween, ser 981	$25–$30
Leap year, p/Gabriel, ser 401	$8–$10
Mirror, ser 30	$6–$8
Smile, ser 169	$5–$6
Smile, ser 169 w/ButterKrust ad	$8–$10
Zodiac valentines, p/Tuck, ser 128	
	$10–$15
EBNER, PAULI	$10–$30

E.D. (*see* Ethel DeWees)

E.H.D. (*see* Ethel DeWees)

ELLAM, WILLIAM (British)	$5–$30
ELLIOTT, KATHRYN (American)	$4–$10
ELYM (political)	$20–$40
FIDLER, ALICE LUELLA (Alice Fidler Person)	
	$8–$15
FIDLER, ELSIE CATHERINE	$8–$15

FIDLER, PEARL EUGENIA (Pearl Fidler Lemunyan)
$8–$15

Courtesy of John and Sandy Milns

Printed credit: "Painted by Alice Luella Fidler." "The American Girl," #120, from a series of nearly 150, copyright by Edward Gross Co., New York. Probably late teens. Not common. Value: $10.

FISHER, HARRISON (American, 1875–1934)

	$10–$30
p/Detroit	$15–$30
p/Reinthal & Newman	$10–$20
Advertising postcards	$75
900 series	$75–$100

From the author's collection

Signed Harrison Fisher. "Their New Love," the last (#191) of the popular six-card series on courtship and marriage. Copyright by Charles Scribner's Sons and published by Reinthal & Newman, New York. Common. Value: $10.

From the author's collection

Signed Harrison Fisher. "Dumb Luck." A beautiful woman and a horse was a common and ever-popular theme. Copyright by Charles Scribner's Sons and published by Reinthal & Newman, New York. Not common. Value: $15.

FLAGG, JAMES MONTGOMERY (American) $5–$15

From the author's collection

Signed James Montgomery Flagg (creator of the World War I recruiting poster of Uncle Sam—"I Want You"). From the mural (originally displayed at Jack Dempsey's restaurant on Broadway in New York City) of the Jack Dempsey–Jess Willard fight that took place July 4, 1919, in Toledo, Ohio. The linen postcard dates from a later decade. Common. Value: $6.

Remember! All prices in this guide represent postcards in *Excellent* condition.

FLOWERS, CHARLES	$5–$10
FREIXAS, JASON	$20–$50
GASSAWAY, KATHARINE (American)	$8–$20

From the author's collection

Signed Katharine Gassaway. "The College Girl," #FL142, copyright 1906, and published by the Rotograph Co., New York. This undivided-back postcard is part of a large series of designs of children playing the roles of various professions. Not common. Value: $8.

GEAR, MABEL $5–$15

Courtesy of John and Sandy Millns

Signed M. Gear. "Polo Ponies, Show Winners" is #5168 of Mabel Gear's Horse Series, published by Valentine. Probably 1930s. Common. Value: $6.

Signed M. Gear. "Master's Footsteps" shows three lovable dogs—a Scotch terrier, springer spaniel, and corgi—peaking through the openings in a gate. From Mabel Gear's Dog Series, #1991, published by Valentine. Probably 1930s. Common. Value: $6.

GEARY, RICK **(American, b. 1946)**   *$1–$10*

Signed Rick Geary. This contemporary illustrator has created dozens of designs for postcard collectors who print personal postcards of their collecting wants, to advertise club shows, or to commemorate the annual National Postcard Week. Common. Value: $2.

The minimum value in this price guide is $1. While many dealers offer 25-cent and 50-cent "bargain boxes," few dealers sort, individually price, and protectively "sleeve" postcards valued at less than $1. This price guide offers values for postcards worth $1 or more.

GIBSON, CHARLES DANA (American, 1867–1944)

$8–$35

p/Detroit, 14,000 series $15–$25

Courtesy of John and Sandy Millns

Signed C. D. Gibson. "Gladys," a beautifully wrought portrait by the illustrator, is credited with idealizing American feminine beauty. Not common. Value: $8.

GREENAWAY, KATHERINE A. (English, 1846–1902)

$60–$100

GREINER, MAGNUS $8–$25

Blacks $20–$25

Dutch children $12–$15

Molly and the Bear series $12–$18

Courtesy of John and Sandy Millns

Signed M. Greiner. "<u>Contemplation</u>" shows two Dutch children playing house. Dutch children are a common ethnic variant on American postcards. Divided back, copyright Knapp Co., New York. Not common. Value: $15.

A Darktown Philosopher.
Der's nuffin half so sweet in life,
    As a watermillion juicy an' fine;
Except to marry
        a charmin' wife,
Jes' like you,
    ma VALENTINE.

From the author's collection

*Signed M. Greiner. A derogatory stereotype was a common treat-
ment of black Americans on postcards, as in this example published by the International Art Pub. Co., New York. The painting
was copyright 1906. Not common.* Value: $20.

GRIGGS, H. B., P/L & E (women and patriotic designs are valued higher than children and pix-
ies) $5–$20
    Christmas $10–$20
    Halloween $15 –$20
GUNN, ARCHIE (American) $8–$20
    p/National Art, u/b, city girls $8–$12

Courtesy of John and Sandy Milins

BLUE BELLE

*Signed Archie Gunn. "Blue Belle," a beautiful woman in a large
hat. Pre–World War I. Not common.* Value: $15.

GUTMANN, BESSIE PEASE (American)   *$15–$40*

Courtesy of John and Sandy Millns

Signed Bessie Pease Gutmann. "Strenuous" shows Teddy Roose-velt's influence on postcard design: the child is playing "rough-rider." Copyright 1907 by Gutmann & Gutmann, published by Reinthal & Newman, cancelled in 1909. Scarce. Value: $25.

H.B.G. (*see* H. B. Griggs)
H.H. (*see* Hermann Hesse)
HARDY, FLORENCE   *$8–$20*

Courtesy of John and Sandy Millns

"HE WHO HESITATES IS LOST."

Signed Florence Hardy. English. Dutch children and skating are the themes of this design, #500B, published by C. W. Faulkner. Not common. Value: $10.

HAYS, MARGARET GEBBIE $20–$40

Courtesy of John and Sandy Millns

Signed M. G. Hays. Margaret G. Hayes was Grace Wiederseim Drayton's sister; their maiden name was Gebbie. Hays' postcard art consisted of drawings of children. The illustration, #3062, a Valentine greeting published by Nister, shows a little girl in an exaggerated hat. Scarce. Value: $30.

HEINMULLER $8–$12
HELLI (*see* Louis Icart)
HEROUARD (French) $10–$20

Courtesy of John and Sandy Millns

Signed Herouard. A young French woman waves an American flag and walks arm-in-arm with an American doughboy. World War I. #273. Not common. Value: $15.

HESSE, HERMANN   *$5–$10*

From the author's collection

Signed H.H. "The Athletic Girl" is from a 30-card series of comic
Vinegar Valentines of ethnic, professional, and behavioral stereo-
types. Copyright 1905, published by Illustrated Post Card Co.
Common. Value: $5.

HORINA, H. (American) $5–$15
HUMPHREY, MAUDE (American) $8–$25

Courtesy of John and Sandy Millns

An unsigned design by Maude Humphrey. Copyright 1909 by L. R.
Conwell. (Signed Maude Humphrey postcards bring a premium.)
This card not common. Value: $8.

HUTAF, AUGUST (American, b. 1879) $5–$15

Signed August Hutaf. A comic design that incorporates three collecting themes—birthdays, children, and fraternal. Copyright 1908
by Ullman Mfg. Co., New York. Not common. Value: $10.

ICART, LOUIS (French)   ——— $60–$125

Signed Helli, nickname for Louis Icart. French. From the Paris
Fashion Series, "Summer Dress." World War I period. Not common. Value: $80.

Remember! All prices in this guide represent postcards in
Excellent condition.

Courtesy of John and Sandy Millns

Signed Louis Icart. #48, a glamour design. Scarce. Value: $100.

INNES, JOHN (Canadian, 1864–1941) $5–$25

J.E.P. (*see* John E. Pitts)

JOHNSON, J. $6–$10

JOSZA, CARL (Art Nouveau) $300–$800

KABER, G. F. (Adventures of Lovely Lilly)

$45–$50

KALVACH, RUDOLF $1,500–$2,000

KEMPF, E. TH. $50–$80

Courtesy of Fred Schiffman

Signed E. Th. Kempf. An angled view of a beautiful woman is incorporated into the multilayered Art Nouveau design. Series 165, #10. Rare. Value: $60.

KENNEDY, A. E. (British) $4–$10

Courtesy of John and Sandy Millns

Signed A. E. Kennedy. A comic illustration of a dog as a bobby.
Published by Faulkner, cancelled in 1913. Not common. Value: $8.

KIMBALL, ALONZO (American, 1874–1923)

$5–$15

Courtesy of John and Sandy Millns

Signed Alonzo Kimball. Fortune telling, courtship, and beautiful
people are the major themes of "Telltale Lines," published by
Reinthal & Newman, copyright 1906 by Charles Scribner's Sons.
Not common. Value: $10.

The minimum value in this price guide is $1. While many
dealers offer 25-cent and 50-cent "bargain boxes," few
dealers sort, individually price, and protectively "sleeve"
postcards valued at less than $1. This price guide offers
values for postcards worth $1 or more.

KING, HAMILTON (American) $8–$20
Bathing beauties, p/Wilcox, ca. 1907

$10–$15
Coke ad card (*see* "Advertising" section
under "Topical Cards")

Signed Hamilton King, 1914. A beautiful ice skater adjusts her skates in this uncommon winter scene. Published by Henry Heininger. Not common. Value: $15.

KINNEYS, THE $8–$15

Signed The Kinneys. A colorful woman in peasant dress playing a tambourine. Copyright Edward Gross, New York, Kinney #7. Not common. Value: $10.

KIRCHNER, RAPHAEL (Austrian, 1876–1917)

	$40–$250
Early work	$80–$250
Hold-to-lights	$250
Invitation to join Paris postcard club	
	$2,000
Later work	$40–$100

From the author's collection

Signed Raphael Kirchner. A fine litho print of a delicately wrought beautiful woman playing with marionettes. The background and decoration are stippled gold. Undivided back. Rare. Value: $120.

From the author's collection

By Raphael Kirchner, unsigned. The swirling lines from the sun's rays, the beautiful woman's hair, and the flower petals and stems all add to the intoxication of this design. Scarce. Value: $80.

KLEIN, CATHARINE $4–$30
   Advertising $10–$30
   Alphabet designs $8–$15
   Flowers $4–$15

Courtesy of John and Sandy Millns

Signed C. Klein. One of the more commonplace floral designs. Value: $4.

KNIGHT, M. $4–$10

Courtesy of John and Sandy Millns

Signed M. Knight and A. E. Kennedy. A cute doggie and a cute verse. That's all the ingredients needed to make a pleasing postcard for many a dog lover! Not common. Value: $8.

KOEHLER, MELA (Austrian, 1885–1960) $30–$300
   Art Deco designs $30–$100
   Wiener Werkstätte designs $100–$300

From the author's collection

Signed Mela Koehler. One of the six-card series of women with dogs and muffs. The colorful detail of the background wallpaper adds to the claustrophobia—and attraction—of the complex design. Rare. Value: $100.

KOKOSCHKA, OSKAR (Austrian, 1886–1980)
                               $500–$3,000
   KYD (Joseph Clayton Clarke, English)
                               $12–$20

Courtesy of John and Sandy Millns

Signed KYD. An example from the twenty-four designs in the Characters From Charles Dickens Series, this is "Toots," series 857 II. An undivided-back card published by Raphael Tuck & Sons. The designs were also issued with divided backs, renumbered. Scarce. Value: $15.

LANDSEER, SIR EDWIN (English, 1802–1873, animals) $4–$15
LARSEN, GARY (American) $1–$2
LARSEN, L. H. ("Dude") $2–$10

Just A Western Line, From You Know, Who

Signed and copyright by L. H. Larsen. An example of Larsen's colorful linens with a western theme, #24, copyright 1944. Common. Value: $2.

LE MAIR, WILLEBEEK $8–$25

Printed credit Willebeek Le Mair. Children's illustration, "The Doves' Dinner Time." Published by Augener, London, 1920s. Not common. Value: $15.

LEYENDECKER, JOSEPH CHRISTINA (German-American, 1874–1951) $15–$50
    u/s Chesterfield advertising $45–$50
    Men's clothing advertising $15–$30
LIKARZ, MARIA $200–$400

LONGLEY, CHILTON $10–$30

Courtesy of John and Sandy Millns

Signed Chilton Longley. Art Deco glamour, series 422, published by AG & G, London. Scarce. Value: $30.

MAILICK, R. (German)	$5–$20
Die-cut hold-to-light	$20–$100
MANNING, REG (American)	$4–$15
M.E.P. M.P. (*see* Margaret E. Price)	
McCAY, WINSOR ZENIE (American, 1869–1934)	
	$20–$30
Little Nemo	$25–$30
McGILL, DONALD (English, 1875–1962, humor)	
	$5–$15
McMANUS, GEORGE (American, 1884–1954)	$20–$40
MEGARGEE, LON (American)	$4–$15

MESCHINI, G. (Italian) $20–$50

Courtesy of John and Sandy Millns

Signed G. Meschini. Italian Art Deco and glamour are the key words for this colorful design! Published in the 1920s or '30s. Scarce. Value: $40.

MEUNIER, HENRI (Belgian) $50–$150

Courtesy of John and Sandy Millns

Signed H. Meunier. "Été" (summer) is an Art Nouveau design with little decoration. Undivided back. Rare. Value: $100.

MEUNIER, SUZANNE (French) $25–$50
MORTON, JOHN (American) $5–$20
MOSER, KOLOMAN (Austrian, 1868–1918)
  $200–$500

MUCHA, ALPHONSE (Czechoslovakian, 1860–1939)

	$50–$12,500
Cocorico	$300–$500
Czechoslovakian designs	$100–$300
Months	$80–$150
Sarah Bernhardt	$100–$200
Waverley Cycles advertising	$12,500

Courtesy of Jonah Shapiro

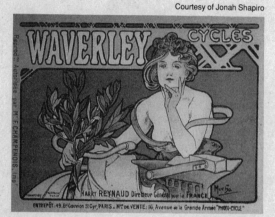

Signed Mucha. An advertising postcard for Waverley Cycles, published in 1898. Only five copies of it are known to exist. Shown here is the top half of a vertically oriented postcard. The bottom half of the card was left blank for a message. This is the most expensive postcard valued for its image alone. Value: An unused pristine card sold for $12,500 in 1990; a second buyer then purchased it for $13,500.

The minimum value in this price guide is $1. While many dealers offer 25-cent and 50-cent "bargain boxes," few dealers sort, individually price, and protectively "sleeve" postcards valued at less than $1. This price guide offers values for postcards worth $1 or more.

MYER **(American)**   **$4–$10**

From the author's collection

CIGARETTE FIEND

Signed Myer. The "Cigarette Fiend," a comic Vinegar Valentine, #A27 of the Aurochrome Series, makes fun of the nicotine addict. Common. Value: $5.

NANNI, GIOVANNI **(Italian, 1888–1969)**   **$20–$40**

Courtesy of John and Sandy Millns

Signed Nanni. A romantic drawing, #373-3, published in the 1920s or '30s. Scarce. Value: $20.

NERMAN (Swedish) $5–$15

Courtesy of John and Sandy Millns

Signed Nerman. An Art Deco-style Swedish New Year's greeting from the 1920s. Not common. Value: $10.

NEWALL, PETER (American, 1862–1924)

$15–$30

NOSWORTHY, FLORENCE ENGLAND $4–$10

Courtesy of Fred Schiffman

Signed Florence England Nosworthy. A charming illustration of children in the garden. Numbered 455, published by F. A. Owen, the card has an embossed edge border. Not common. Value: $6.

NYSTROM, JENNY (Swedish, 1854–1946)

$5–$50

O'NEILL, ROSE (American, 1874–1944)

$15–$150

Blacks ("American humor from Puck"),
p/Tuck $100
Kewpies, p/Gibson $40–$60
Kewpies, unsigned $15–$20
"Klever Kards" (easle-back), p/Campbell
Art $35–$55
Rock Island RR advertising $50–$75
Suffrage, p/Campbell Art $150
Suffrage, p/National Woman Suffrage

$300

OPPER, FREDERICK BURR (American, 1857–1937)

$5–$15

From the author's collection

Signed F. Opper. Newspaper cartoon characters Alphonse and Gaston. (Opper's other major character reproduced on postcards was the Happy Hooligan.) Copyright 1906 by the American Journal Examiner. Scarce. Value: $10.

OUTCAULT, RICHARD FELTON (American 1863–1928)

$10–$75
Buster Brown $10–$30
Rockford Watch calendars $15–$30
Yellow Kid $50–$75

OUTHWAITE, IDA R. (Australian, 1889–1961)

$15–$25

Courtesy of John and Sandy Milins

Drawing and story by Ida R. Outhwaite, "The Witch's Sister," Elves and Fairies Series, #76. Published by A & C Black, London. Cancelled in 1931. Scarce. Value: $20.

PARKINSON, ETHEL

$8–$15

Courtesy of John and Sandy Milins

Signed Ethel Parkinson. A winter scene of a girl with a basket of holly. Cancelled in 1906. Not common. Value: $12.

PARRISH, MAXFIELD (American, 1870–1966)

$40–$100

PAYNE, HARRY (English, 1858–1927)   *$10–$50*
    The Wild West, p/Tuck, ser 2630   *$15–$20*
    Military designs   *$10–$20*

Courtesy of John and Sandy Millns

Printed credit to Harry Payne. "The Racer," published by Raphael Tuck, shows the concentration of the race horse by its flared nostrils, engorged veins, and staring eyes. An early undivided-back postcard, issued in 1898, this example was cancelled in 1902. Rare. Value: $40.

PEASE, BESSIE COLLINS (*see* Bessie Pease Gutmann)

Courtesy of John and Sandy Millns

Signed Bessie Collins Pease. Two little girls have a "Falling Out." Copyright 1907 by Gutmann & Gutmann, published by Reinthal & Newman. Scarce. Value: $25.

PELTIER, L. **(French)**   *$10–$25*

Courtesy of John and Sandy Milins

Credited on the back: "par L. Peltier." A risqué vision of an attractive woman as she bends to retrieve her fallen pocketbook, whose dress has blown up revealing all! Series #8–37. Not common. Value: $15.

PENFIELD, EDWARD **(American)**   *$15–$20*

From the author's collection

Signed Edward Penfield. "The Buffalo Pen, Bronx Park Zoo, New York" is one in a series of advertising cards, copyright by Hart Schaffner & Marx. Pre–World War I. Scarce. Value: $20.

PEPIN, MAURICE (French) $8–$20

Courtesy of John and Sandy Millns

Signed Maurice Pepin. A glamour/erotic design. 1920s? Not common. Value: $15.

PEW, GERTRUDE	$6–$8
PHILLIPS, COLES (American, 1880–1927)	$20–$40
Advertising	$20–$40
Fadeaway	$20–$30
PITTS, JOHN E. (American)	$6–$15
PRICE, MARGARET E.	$4–$15
Halloween greetings	$8–$15
RALPH, LESTER (American, 1877–1927)	$10–$20

Courtesy of John and Sandy Millns

Signed Lester Ralph. In "An Offer of Affection" a beautiful young woman puts aside her book to play with her dog, #302–2, copyright by the Knapp Co. (K. Co.), New York, and published by Paul Heckscher, Inc. Scarce. Value: $15.

REMINGTON, FREDERIC S. (American, 1861–1909)

$40–$80

Signed Frederic Remington. "Evening on a Canadian"; two men and a dog canoeing. The postcard is design #14179 published by Detroit Pub. Co., copyright 1905 by Collier's. Rare. Value: $60.

ROBINSON, FLORENCE $15–$25

Signed Florence Robinson. "Wall Street" from the fine litho-printed series of artist-drawn views published by Raphael Tuck & Sons. Robinson produced series (not all signed) for several American cities. Private mailing card back. Scarce. Value: $20.

ROBINSON, ROBERT **(American, 1886–1952)**

$20–$60

Courtesy of John and Sandy Milins

Signed Robt. Robinson. A young boy winds up to pitch a ball. From the Robert Robinson Series 208, copyright and published by Edward Gross. Not common. Value: $35.

ROBINSON, WALLACE **(American)** $10–$20

Courtesy of Fred Schiffman

Signed W.R. "He Played Villa!" is from a series of four patriotic cards of children at play. Copyright Henry Heininger Co., New York. This is the most desirable of the four. Scarce. Value: $20.

ROCKWELL, NORMAN (American, 1894–1978)

$20–$80

Fatherless Children $35
Fisk Tires $20–$25

Signed Norman Rockwell. A World War II patriotic design. Scarce. Value: $35.

RUSNAK, ANN (American) $1–$3
RUSSELL, CHARLES MARION (American, 1865–1926)

$10–$25

p/W. T. Ridgley calendars $10–$15

Courtesy of John and Sandy Millns

Signed C.M.R. 1907. The cattle skull was a characteristic part of Russell's signed initials. Published by the W. T. Ridgley Calendar Co. Russell's paintings have been reproduced on postcards by museums up to the present contemporary issues. Value: $15.

RUSSELL, MARY LA FENETRA $5–$15
Halloween, p/Gabriel $8–$15

RYAN, E. (American)   *$5–$25*

Courtesy of John and Sandy Millns

Signed Ryan. "Curiosity," #C635 from the popular Fantasy Ladies Series, clearly shows Ryan's Art Nouveau style. Scarce. Value: $25.

RYLANDER   *$10–$20*

Courtesy of John and Sandy Millns

Signed Rylander. This postcard is a fine example of European Art Deco. Scarce. Value: $15.

S.L.S (*see* Samuel L. Schmucker)

Remember! All prices in this guide represent postcards in *Excellent* condition.

SAGER, XAVIER (French) $20–$50
        Early period $20–$50
        Later period $20–$30

Signed Xavier Sager. Sager was a prolific creator of erotic/ glamour postcards. Here's a French woman with Uncle Sam as a cock looks on. Not common. Value: $25.

SANDFORD, M. DIX (English) $10–$20

Courtesy of John and Sandy Millns

Signed M. Dix Sandford. An Oilette design from Raphael Tuck's Seaside Coons Series #9318. Not common. Value: $10.

SCHMUCKER, SAMUEL L. (American) $35–$250
    Butterfly series, p/Detroit $150
    Childhood Days series, p/Detroit $200
    Drinks series, p/Detroit $150
    Fairy Queen series, p/Detroit $200
    Halloween series 100, p/Tuck (unsigned)
                       $30–$35
    Halloween, p/Winsch $40–$150
    Mermaids series, p/Detroit $150
    p/National Art, soldiers' greetings (unsigned) $75
    National Girls series, p/Detroit $125–$150
    Smokes series, p/Detroit $150

Courtesy of John and Sandy Millns

Signed S.L.S. The initials appear to the right and under the top swirl of smoke halfway between the cigar and the woman's chin. "Lucinda" is one of four designs by Schmucker in the Smokes Series published by Detroit Pub. Co. Undivided back. Rare. Value: $150.

A Schmucker design, "Sherry," in the Drinks Series published by Detroit Pub. Co.; the artist's initials are not visible. Rare. Value: $150.

SHAND, C. E. (English) $5–$15

Signed C.E. Shand. "The Flower Girl" shows a woman in 19th-century dress. Not common. Value: $15.

The minimum value in this price guide is $1. While many dealers offer 25-cent and 50-cent "bargain boxes," few dealers sort, individually price, and protectively "sleeve" postcards valued at less than $1. This price guide offers values for postcards worth $1 or more.

SHINN, COBB (American, 1887–1951) *$5–$15*
SMITH, JESSIE WILLCOX (American, 1863–1935)
$15–$25

Courtesy of John and Sandy Milins

Signed Jessie Willcox Smith. This is one of six highly desirable designs. Copyright by Charles Scribner's Sons, published by Reinthal & Newman. Common. Value: $20.

de SOLOMKO, S. *$15–$25*

Courtesy of John and Sandy Milins

Signed Solomko. "Neuf mois apres!" (Nine months later!); a child in a bed of Easter lilies pops out of an egg! #2434 from IML (Paris). Post–World War I. Not common. Value: $20.

SOWERBY, MILLICENT (English, 1878–1967)

$10–$25

Courtesy of John and Sandy Millns

Signed M. Sowerby. "Flowers and Wings." A desirable card for collectors of fairy tales and elves. Not common. Value: $10.

Courtesy of Fred Schiffman

Signed Millicent Sowerby, 1911. "Wet"; a solemn-faced girl with a very large umbrella. Not common. Value: $10.

SPURGIN, FRED (children), p/Bamforth $5–$15

ST. JOHN $4–$15

STANSLAWS, PENRHYN (American) $10–$25

Courtesy of John and Sandy Millns

Signed Penrhyn Stanslaws. A young woman in a middy blouse and large hat. Copyright Edward Gross Co., New York. Numbered 8, from the late teens or early 1920s. Not common. Value: $15.

STEIN, GEORGES (French), "Woman in Paris," u/b
series $5–$8
STENBERG, AINA (Swedish) $15–$20
TAM, JEAN (French) $10–$25

Courtesy of John and Sandy Millns

Signed Jean Tam. Series 75, #6; "Les Baigneuses" shows a slim young woman in a very tight bathing suit and bathing slippers on a diving board. Early 1920s. Not common. Value: $15.

TARRANT, MARGARET (English, 1888–1959)

$5–$15

TEMPEST, DOUGLAS (English) $2–$10

Signed D. Tempest. A knock-kneed, smiling, bright-eyed, bulging-cheeked child holds a black kitten in each arm. Published by Bamforth; one of the Tempest Kiddy Series, #K36. Probably post–World War I. Common. Value: $3.

THACKERY, LANCE (English) $8–$20

THIELE, ARTHUR (Dutch, 1841–1916) $10–$40

Signed Arth. Thiele. Known for his depiction of cats. A divided-back postcard, cancelled in 1909. Value: $10.

All values for color plates represent postcards in *Mint* condition. *Photos courtesy of Jonah Shapiro.*

EUROPEAN ART NOUVEAU

Alphonse Mucha. "Cocorico," $500.

Maria Likarz. Wiener Werkstätte #558, $350.

Kirchner. Advertising, Byrrh Tonic, $300.

Unknown artist. Advertising, Karlsruhe perfume factory of F. Wolff & Sohn, $85.

1900 Paris Exposition. From a numbered set of cards in a booklet of thirty passes to various attractions. Value of postcard with ticket attached, $100.

Unknown artist. Poster-style advertising, Englebert Tires, $75.

E. Schneider. Advertising for J. Fischer pâtés de foie gras, $125.

Koloman Moser. Advertising postcard for the postcard publisher Philippe & Kramer's exhibit booth at the 1900 Paris Exposition. Rare, $350.

Unknown artist. Japanese Art Nouveau, excellent example of Secession style, $50.

Toulouse Lautrec, $500.

Rudolf Kalvach. Wiener Werkstätte #49, $1,800.

Vittorio Zecchin. Series IX, #3, $200.

Oskar Kokoschka. Wiener Werkstätte #21, $2,000.

RARE AMERICAN POSTCARDS

Advertising overprint for the American Souvenir Postcard Co. on one of its own "Patriographic" pioneer view cards. Very rare, $100.

Advertising postcard for The Broadmoor Hotel, Colorado Springs. The painting is by Maxfield Parrish. Divided back postcard, $50.

An American "Gruss aus" for the 1897 Schwabischen Fest in Brooklyn. A privately printed "mailing card," copyright 1897 by Edw. Lowey, N.Y., $150.

Advertising for Bull Durham tobacco. "Mexico," from the Around the World series, $50.

Marks-Fram Company's "Main Post Card Exchange" on South Main Street in Los Angeles. The front windows contain displays for California views, foreign views, animals, and comics. Published by Newman Post Card Co., $75.

Advertising for Cribari vineyards, 1939 linen postcard, $35.

Official postcard for the 1913 Armory Art Show, which introduced modern art to the United States, $250.

The artist/signed Philip Boileau, 1906, image of a woman in white with blue hat is repeated five times on the design. Advertising postcard for Flood & Conklin Co., varnish makers, Newark, New Jersey. Copyright 1907, Flood & Conklin, $150.

Pioneer view of the Metropolitan Museum of Art. This was card #1, published by Arthur Livingston. The same design was reprinted with private mailing card and postcard backs. Pioneer, $65; private mailing card, $25; postcard, $10.

Pioneer view of the Statue of Liberty. An 1897 "souvenir" card, #105, published by Ferdinand Strauss, $100.

Suffrage Christmas Greeting. A "Votes for Women" Santa Claus, $85.

Signed by the artist C. M. Russell. Copyright 1905, Brown & Bigelow. Calendar for April 1907. Advertising for Martindale Mercantile Agency, $150.

Santa Claus is used to promote the Simplex typewriter, sold at the Henry R. Johnson store in Springfield, Massachusetts. Divided back postcard, $60.

View card of the printing factory for postcard publisher Hugh C. Leighton Co., $50.

Courtesy of Fred Schiffman

Signed Arth. Thiele. An example from one of the most desirable series. Value: $35.

THOMPSON, NYLA (American, b. 1928)   *$2–$10*
TWELVETREES, CHARLES H. (d. 1948)   *$2–$12*

Courtesy of John and Sandy Millns

Unsigned, printed credit to C. H. Twelvetrees. A cute child, comic #156, copyright Edward Gross Co., New York, from the 1920s or '30s. Common. Value: $3.

Remember! All prices in this guide represent postcards in *Excellent* condition.

UNDERWOOD, CLARENCE F. (American) $12–$25

Courtesy of John and Sandy Millns

Signed Clarence F. Underwood. "Pleasant Reflections"; a woman wearing a hat glances in mirror as she is about to go out. Copyright and published by Reinthal & Newman, New York, this example is from the Watercolor Series 350. Not common. Value: $15.

UPTON, FLORENCE KATE (American, 1873–1922)
$30–$60
VARGAS (Peruvian, b. 1896 Joaquin A. Vargas y Chavez) $30–$50

Courtesy of Fred Schiffman

Signed S. Vargas. Erotic, glamorous women of the 1930s and '40s, Vargas' designs were printed on oversize stock. Scarce. Value: $30.

VEENFLIET, R. (American) $5–$15

Signed R. Veenfliet. One of several patriotic series, #52768, copyright 1909 by S. Garre; embossed, printed in Germany. Common. Value: $8.

VON HARTMANN, EVELYN (greetings)	$3–$8
W.R. (*see* Wallace Robinson)	
WAIN, LOUIS (English, 1860–1939)	$30–$400
Cats	$30–$400
Paper doll cats, Tuck ser 3385	
	$300–$400
Santa Claus cats	$100–$250

A Rose between two Thorns!

Signed Louis Wain. "A Rose Between Two Thorns." Every one of Wain's cat designs is different and desirable; #3021, published by J. Salmon. Scarce. Value: $40.

Signed Louis Wain. The Santa Claus cats are sought after by Santa collectors as well as by Wain and cat collectors. Very rare. Value: $250.

WALL, BERNARD E. (American, 1872–1956)

	$3–$20
Suffrage	$15–$20
Sunbonnets	$12–$20

Signed Wall. The "Votes for Women" has a companion anti-suffrage series where the "wo" in women is blocked out and appropriate negative illustrations and captions are employed. Ca. 1909. Scarce. Value: $20.

WARDLE, ARTHUR   *$5–$15*

Signed Arthur Wardle. "Smooth Basset Hounds." A fine image for dog lovers. Published by A. Vivian Mansell. Value: $8.

WELLMAN, WALTER (American)	$5–$35
Suffragette series	$30–$35
WIEDERSEIM, GRACE GEBBIE (Grace Drayton)	
	$10–$100
Campbell Kids	$60–$100
p/Reinthal & Newman	$10–$25
adv/Swift Pride soap	$30–$40

Signed G.G. Wiederseim. Copyright and published in 1909 by Reinthal & Newman, series 99. Not common. Value: $15.

ZIM (*see* H. G. Zimmerman)
ZIMMERMAN, H. G. (American)   *$3–$15*

Topical Cards

This section of the price guide lists postcards by popular topic. It is divided into ten major groupings. Within each grouping, the subtopics and series, as well as individual titles, artists, and subjects, are listed alphabetically. Subtopics may be further broken down by time period when appropriate.

Collecting by topic crosses over into all of the other categories of postcards. Whether the topic is wildlife, fairy tales, military history, or women's suffrage, for example, appealing and desirable postcards can be found among views, artist-signed postcards, and greetings. Illustrations in all sections of the price guide may apply to topical postcards and vice versa.

Market values for individual examples as well as for the general listings were determined by compiling prices of postcards at shows, from dealers' personal communications, and from estimated values and prices realized in published auctions and fixed price sales. All values are for postcards in Excellent condition.

The ten major groupings of topicals are as follows:

1. Advertising, Commerce, and Industry
2. Entertainment
3. Expositions, Fairs, and Dated Events
4. Family, People, and Everyday Life
5. Fantasy, Glamour, and Erotica
6. History and Politics
7. Miscellaneous
8. Nature, and Basic and Applied Science

ADVERTISING, COMMERCE, AND INDUSTRY

Advertising postcards promote a specific company's product or service. Advertising postcards from all time periods are avidly collected. High demand has greatly reduced the supply of the better cards. First-rate graphic design is particularly sought after. Many collectors find the poster-style especially desirable.

An advertising postcard usually commands a premium over the value of the topic itself. An artist-signed advertising postcard is usually valued higher than a similar design by the same artist that does not promote a product. An advertising postcard incorporating a holiday greeting may be valued higher than a similar greeting without an advertising tie-in.

An advertising imprint added to a previously-printed card often will not command a premium value. For example, many view cards as well as some artist-drawn and greeting cards can be found with an advertiser's name added over the picture or in the message space.

For advertising postcards, more than for most others, chance has been a factor in the number of postcards of any particular design which have survived. When used in bulk mail ad campaigns, the card's purpose was to promote a product, service, or event, and though large numbers may have been mailed, the number that fell into the hands of collectors could be very low.

Because many advertising cards are available only postally used, the range of conditions acceptable to collectors is sometimes broader. However, condition is a significant factor for those early unmailed advertising sets and series which accompanied a product or could be obtained upon request or with a coupon or small payment. Collectors sought these items specifically for collecting, and they have survived in better condition and in greater numbers.

Mid-century advertising postcards, particularly for motels and restaurants, were produced in vast quantities and were widely disseminated free of charge. These usually can be obtained unused in Mint or Near Mint condition. The large supply keeps prices low even for high-quality designs and printing.

In addition to the examples in this section, there are illustrations of advertising postcards in the views, greetings, artist-signed, and other topicals sections.

For more detailed lists of early-century advertising postcards, see Frederick and Mary Megson's *American Advertising Postcards, Sets and Series, 1890–1920, A Catalog and Price Guide*, Martinsville, NJ: The Postcard Lovers, 1985.

ADVERTISING, COMMERCE, AND INDUSTRY VALUES

ADVERTISING (pio. issues)	$20–$500
AIRLINE TRAVEL (m.c.)	$5–$25
AIRLINE TRAVEL (l.c.)	$2–$10
Albert-Hayes Hosiery (e.c.)	$12–$15
Allentown ad postals (e.c.)	$20–$40
American Journal Examiner, mechanicals	$15–$20
Armour Meats, American Girl series	$15–$20
AUTOMOBILES (e.c.)	$10–$50

Courtesy of John and Sandy Millns

Real photo advertising card for the Overland model 61–F. Value: $40.

AUTOMOBILES (m.c.)	$4–$30
AUTOMOBILES (l.c.)	$1–$6

BANKS/S & L'S (e.c.)   *$2–$12*
BANKS/S & L'S (m.c.)   *$2–$10*
BANKS/S & L'S (l.c.)   *$1–$5*
Barnum & Bailey Circus (e.c.)   *$10–$35*
Beardsley's Shredded Codfish (pio. NY views)
    $20–$30
BEER/BREWERIES (e.c.)   *$10–$100*
BEER/BREWERIES (m.c.)   *$2–$25*
BEER/BREWERIES (l.c.)   *$1–$10*
Bell Telephone (e.c.)   *$12–$15*
Bensdorp Royal Dutch Cocoa (e.c.)   *$5–$25*
Berry Brothers Varnish (e.c.)   *$6–$10*
BICYCLES (e.c.)   *$3–$10*
    Waverley Cycles (1898 French ed, s/Mucha)
    $12,000
BICYCLES (m.c.)   *$2–$10*
BICYCLES (l.c.)   *$1–$5*
BOOKS/MAGAZINES (e.c.)   *$1–$5*
BOOKS/MAGAZINES (m.c.)   *$1–$5*
BOOKS/MAGAZINES (l.c.)   *$1–$2*
Boston Rubber Shoes (e.c., views of Boston)
    $4–$8
Buchan's Soap (e.c., with teddy bears) *$20–$25*
Bull Durham Tobacco "Trip around . . ." (e.c.)
    $30–$50
Buster Brown character (e.c.)   *$10–$25*
Byrrh Tonic (e.c.)   *$100–$300*
CAMERAS/PHOTOGRAPHY (e.c.)   *$5–$80*
CAMERAS/PHOTOGRAPHY (m.c.)   *$3–$25*
CAMERAS/PHOTOGRAPHY (l.c.)   *$1–$10*

The minimum value in this price guide is $1. While many dealers offer 25-cent and 50-cent "bargain boxes," few dealers sort, individually price, and protectively "sleeve" postcards valued at less than $1. This price guide offers values for postcards worth $1 or more.

Campbell's Soups (vertical designs)

$90–$100

Campbell's Soups (horizontal designs)

$40–$50

Courtesy of Joel Edler

The Campbell's Soups advertising postcards are unsigned Grace Wiederseim Drayton designs. One of four different horizontal designs. Scarce. Value: $50.

Courtesy of John and Sandy Milns

The vertical Campbell's Soups designs are rare. Value: $100.

CANDY/CHOCOLATES (pio.) $10–$50

Remember! All prices in this guide represent postcards in *Excellent* condition.

CANDY/CHOCOLATES (e.c.) $5–$50

A colorful and delightful design advertising Loose-Wiles stick candy. Mailed by a sales rep in March 1909 from Emporia, Kansas, to Marion, Texas. Rare. Value: $60.

CANDY/CHOCOLATES (m.c.) $5–$15
CANDY/CHOCOLATES (l.c.) $1–$5
J. I. Case farm equipment (e.c.) $6–$12

One of many ad cards issued by the J. I. Case Threshing Machine Co. of Racine, Wisconsin, showing early motorized equipment for agriculture. The eagle perched on globe logo appears on many Case designs. This card shows a steam engine and steel separator available for $880. Common. Value: $8.

"Celebrated Posters" p/Tuck $40–$80

Cherry Smash (e.c.) $200–$300

Courtesy of *Postcard Collector*

An ad card for Fowler's Cherry Smash that is as appetizing as the drink was reputed to be. Another card shows Mt. Vernon. A rare card. Value: $300.

Chesterfield Cigarettes (e.c. uns/Leyendecker)
         $40–$50
Chicago & Alton RR (1904 World's Fair)
         $20–$30

Cinerama (m.c.)	$3–$10
CIRCUS (e.c.)	$5–$30
CIRCUS (m.c.)	$2–$10
CIRCUS (l.c.)	$1–$5
COCA-COLA (e.c.)	$300–$500
COCA-COLA (m.c.)	$10–$80
COCA-COLA (l.c.)	$1–$15
COFFEE (e.c.)	$5–$20
COFFEE (m.c.)	$2–$10
COFFEE (l.c.)	$1–$3
COSMETICS/PERFUME (e.c.)	$3–$20
COSMETICS/PERFUME (m.c.)	$2–$15
COSMETICS/PERFUME (l.c.)	$1–$3

Cracker Jack Bears (e.c.) $25–$30

Courtesy of Joel Edler

No. 3, from the popular series of twenty Cracker Jack Bears, copyright 1907 by B. E. Moreland; shows the bears going over Niagara Falls. These cards measure 3 × 5½ inches. Not common. Value: $25.

DAIRY PRODUCTS/DAIRIES (e.c.)	$5–$15
DAIRY PRODUCTS/DAIRIES (m.c.)	$2–$10

From the author's collection

Alice in Dairyland poses with the "world's largest cheese." A chrome-finish ad card promoting Wisconsin cheese at the Los Angeles County Fair. Not common. Value: $2.

DAIRY PRODUCTS/DAIRIES (l.c.)	$1–$3
DEPARTMENT STORES (e.c.)	$3–$15
DEPARTMENT STORES (m.c.)	$2–$10
DEPARTMENT STORES (l.c.)	$1–$5

DuPont Powders (birds, e.c.)	$50–$60
DuPont Powders (dogs, e.c.)	$60–$75

Courtesy of *Postcard Collector*

The ruffed grouse, an example from the DuPont Powders series of twelve wild game illustrations. Scarce. Value: $55.

Edison Phonographs (e.c., famous singers)	
	$25–$30
FARM EQUIPMENT/MACHINERY (e.c.)	$5–$25
Real photo advertising	$10–$40
FARM EQUIPMENT/MACHINERY (m.c.)	$2–$8
FARM EQUIPMENT/MACHINERY (l.c.)	$1–$5
5A Horse Blankets (e.c.)	$15–$20
Fisk Tires (e.c.)	$20–$25
FOOD/FOOD PRODUCTS (e.c.)	$5–$20
FOOD/FOOD PRODUCTS (m.c.)	$2–$10

Courtesy of Joel Edler

Appetizing chrome-finish view of Kroger's produce section. The postcard was mailed at the bulk rate and is a coupon redeemable for five pounds of sugar. Scarce. Value: $5.

FOOD/FOOD PRODUCTS (l.c.) $1–$3
Fralinger's Saltwater Taffy (e.c.) $10–$30
     Nursery rhymes s/C. M. Burd $25–$30
Frisco System RR (1904 World's Fair)
                         $20–$25
Frog in Your Throat Troches (e.c.) $30–$40
Gold Dust Twins Soap (e.c.) $40–$60
Hart Schaffner Marx (e.c., s/Edward Penfield)
                         $15–$20
Heinz Foods (e.c.) $8–$20
Hershey Chocolates (e.c.) $4–$8

Courtesy of Joel Edler

Dozens of views of the manufacturing process and employee facilities were issued as ad cards by the Hershey Chocolate Co. This one shows the cocoa roasters. Printed in green and black on white, the cards measure 2¾ × 5⅝ inches. Common. Value: $5.

Hershey Chocolates (m.c.) $2–$5
Hershey Chocolates (l.c.) $1–$2

The minimum value in this price guide is $1. While many dealers offer 25-cent and 50-cent "bargain boxes," few dealers sort, individually price, and protectively "sleeve" postcards valued at less than $1. This price guide offers values for postcards worth $1 or more.

HOME APPLIANCES (e.c.)	$5–$35
HOME APPLIANCES (m.c.)	$2–$20

A rare linen-finish advertising card issued by Sears Roebuck for the gold-seal Coldspot electric refrigerator. Postally used 1939 from Pittsburgh, Pennsylvania, a hand-written message on the back invites the recipient to visit the store. Rare. Value: $15

HOME APPLIANCES (l.c.)	$1–$5
HOME FURNISHINGS (e.c.)	$5–$25
HOME FURNISHINGS (m.c.)	$2–$15
HOME FURNISHINGS (l.c.)	$1–$10
HOTELS (pio.)	$20–$50
HOTELS (e.c.)	$3–$15
HOTELS (m.c.)	$1–$10
HOTELS (l.c.)	$1–$2
Huyler's Candies (e.c.)	$5–$15
INSURANCE (e.c.)	$5–$25
INSURANCE (m.c.)	$2–$10
INSURANCE (l.c.)	$1–$3

JOB CIGARETTES (e.c.)   *$100–$300*

Courtesy of *Postcard Collector*

Artist-signed Mucha, from the Collection Job Series advertising Job Cigarettes. Very rare. Value: $300.

Courtesy of *Postcard Collector*

Artist signed C. Leandre, from the Collection Job Series advertising Job Cigarettes. Very rare. Value: $100.

Courtesy of *Postcard Collector*

Artist-signed P. Gervais, from the Collection Job Series advertising Job Cigarettes. Very rare. Value: $100.

Johnson Motors (m.c.) $5–10

WHERE THERE'S A *SeaHorse* THERE'S FUN

Johnson Motors of Waukegan, Illinois, advertised their SeaHorse outboard motors on color postcards of action photos made on Kodachrome film. 1940s? Not common. Value: $10.

Kellogg's (e.c.)	$15–$20
Kellogg's (m.c.)	$3–$8
Kellogg's (l.c.)	$1–$2
Kornelia Kinks (H.O. Cereals, e.c.)	$10–$12

"You smash dem Kinks
I'll spoil you' face chile"

One of the three common red and black Korn Kinks designs. (On the rare design, the kite is in the air—as on this one—but there is no five cents on the building.) On the other two designs the kite is on the ground. Value: common designs, $12; rare design, $30.

McDonald's (m.c.)   *$10–$20*

From the author's collection

McDonald's is now an international institution. In the 1960s— before "Big Macs" and when hamburgers only cost 15 cents— advertising postcards helped promote the drive-in's products. A scarce postcard. Value: $10.

McDonald's (l.c.)	*$1–$10*
MEDICINES/REMEDIES (e.c.)	*$3–$30*
MEDICINES/REMEDIES (m.c.)	*$2–$15*
MEDICINES/REMEDIES (l.c.)	*$1–$3*
MEN'S FASHIONS (e.c.)	*$5–$25*
Unsigned Leyendecker	*$20–$40*
MEN'S FASHIONS (m.c.)	*$2–$30*
MEN'S FASHIONS (l.c.)	*$1–$3*
Metropolitan Life Insurance (e.c.)	*$6–$10*
MOTELS (m.c.)	*$2–$20*

Courtesy of Joel Edler

Motels are one of the most common subjects on linen-finish post-cards of the 1930s, '40s, and '50s. Only the most unusual support high values. This one shows two interiors and an overview of Wig-wam Village No. 6 located in Holbrook, Arizona, produced by Curt Teich Co. in 1951. Scarce. Value: $15.

MOTELS (l.c.)   *$1–$5*

MOTORCYCLES (e.c.)	$5–$20
Real photo	$15–$50
MOTORCYCLES (m.c.)	$3–$15
MOTORCYCLES (l.c.)	$2–$8
MOVIES, PLAYS, THEATER (e.c.)	$5–$20
MOVIES, PLAYS, THEATER (m.c.)	$2–$15
MOVIES, PLAYS, THEATER (l.c.)	$1–$5
MOXIE (e.c.)	$60–$80
MUSICAL INSTRUMENTS (e.c.)	$3–$20
MUSICAL INSTRUMENTS (m.c.)	$3–$10
MUSICAL INSTRUMENTS (l.c.)	$1–$5
New York Herald (e.c., Lovely Lilly)	$45–$50
NEWSPAPERS (e.c.)	$3–$15
NEWSPAPERS (m.c.)	$1–$10
NEWSPAPERS (l.c.)	$1–$2
NURSERIES/SEEDS (e.c.)	$3–$10
NURSERIES/SEEDS (m.c.)	$1–$10
NURSERIES/SEEDS (l.c.)	$1–$5
OFFICE EQUIPMENT (e.c.)	$4–$15
OFFICE EQUIPMENT (m.c.)	$2–$10
OFFICE EQUIPMENT (l.c.)	$1–$5
Quaddy Playthings Co. (e.c.)	$20–$25
RAIL TRANSPORT (e.c.)	$3–$15
RAIL TRANSPORT (m.c.)	$1–$10
RAIL TRANSPORT (l.c.)	$1–$5
RCA VICTOR (m.c., big-band leaders)	$6–$12
RESTAURANTS (e.c.)	$3–$10

The minimum value in this price guide is $1. While many dealers offer 25-cent and 50-cent "bargain boxes," few dealers sort, individually price, and protectively "sleeve" postcards valued at less than $1. This price guide offers values for postcards worth $1 or more.

RESTAURANTS (m.c.) $1–$10

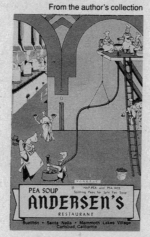

From the author's collection

A colorful poster-style design and a delightful subject. Also, a "great card that isn't," because it's common. Hundreds of thousands of copies have been given to patrons at Andersen's restaurants over several decades. One can even collect varities! Value: $1–$2.

RESTAURANTS (l.c.) $1–$3

ROCK & ROLL CONCERTS (l.c.) $10–$20

Rock Island Lines RR (e.c., s/O'Neill)

$50–$75

Rockford Watch Co. (e.c. calenders, s/Outcault)

$20–$25

Royal Garden Teas dressing dolls (e.c.)

$40–$50

Sambo's Restaurants (1960s) $4

p/Schmidt (general artwork for ad cards)

$10–$100

SEWING MACHINES/SUPPLIES (e.c.) $10–$20

SEWING MACHINES/SUPPLIES (m.c.) $2–$10

SEWING MACHINES/SUPPLIES (l.c.) $1–$5

SHOES/BOOTS (e.c.) $5–$25

SHOES/BOOTS (m.c.) $5–$20

SHOES/BOOTS (l.c.) $1–$5

Sleepy Eye Milling Co. (e.c.)   *$50–$80*

*"This is one of a series of nine beautiful Indian post cards" is printed at the top of this ad card for Sleepy Eye, the Meritorious Flour. **Rare**. Value: $80.*

SOAP (e.c.)	$1–$5
STOVES (e.c.)	$15–$20
Swift's Butterine/Oleomargarine (e.c.)	
	$10–$20
Swift's Meats (e.c.)	$5–$8
Swift's Pride Soap (e.c., shadows)	$15–$20
Swift's Pride Soap (children, s/Wiederseim)	
	$30–$40
TEA (e.c.)	$7–$15
TIRES (e.c.)	$10–$25
TOBACCO/CIGARETTES (e.c.)	$10–$60
TOBACCO/CIGARETTES (m.c.)	$2–$20
TOBACCO/CIGARETTES (l.c.)	$1–$3
Tupperware (l.c.)	$1–$5
Vin Fiz Grape Drink (Roger's Flight)	$75
Walkover Shoes (e.c.)	$5–$15
WINES/WINERIES (e.c.)	$7–$30
WINES/WINERIES (m.c.)	$2–$10
WINES/WINERIES (l.c.)	$1–$3
WOMEN'S FASHIONS (e.c.)	$5–$30
WOMEN'S FASHIONS (m.c.)	$2–$20
WOMEN'S FASHIONS (l.c.)	$1–$5
Woonsocket Rubber Co. (Footwear of Nations)	
	$5–$10

Wyandott Cleanser (e.c.)   *$8–$15*
Yellow Kid character (e.c., s/R. F. Outcault)
     $50–$75
Zeno Chewing Gum (e.c.)   *$3–$10*
Zeno Chewing Gum (1904 World's Fair, p/Tuck)
     $18–$20

ENTERTAINMENT

Postcards themselves are entertainment. Postcards of entertainment subjects have wide appeal.

Movie stars and movie advertising on postcards are a steady favorite. Entertainers from the 1930s and '40s on arcade cards with postcard backs enjoy increasing demand. Marilyn Monroe is a perennial favorite; modern cards of Monroe produced in the 1980s and '90s are as avidly collected (though lower priced) as older cards from the 1950s and '60s. Linen-style postcards of Hollywood stars with their homes are avidly sought.

Stage actors, actresses, theaters, and theater advertising have a dedicated following. In an upper stratum are Mucha-designed ad cards for Sarah Bernhardt. Early television personalities are also gaining a following.

Amusement parks are avidly collected. Most asked for are the carousels; real photos bring a high premium. Circus performers and advertising, and early Wild West show postcards also have strong support.

Americana of all periods and roadside attractions of mid-century production are eagerly sought. Postcards showing an Uncle Sam character rank highest in value.

Diners, lunch wagons, popcorn wagons, and similar subjects—especially on real photo postcards—have enthusiastic followers.

Sports entertainment on postcards is spotty. Real photos of hometown baseball teams are eagerly sought. Early postcards of professional baseball teams, especially championship teams, are strong. Postcards of individual baseball players may track the values of their companion baseball cards.

Autos, horses, and racing are all popular topics.

Jazz musicians and big band entertainers on mid-century postcards are increasing in value. Demand continues to grow for advertising postcards from 1960s–'70s rock concerts. Elvis and the Beatles each have their specialist collectors.

In the listings which follow, the abbreviations, e.c. = early-century, m.c. = mid-century, and l.c. = late-century refer to the age of the postcard, not the age of the person or event.

ENTERTAINMENT VALUES

ACTORS/ACTRESSES (e.c.)	$8–$20
ACTORS/ACTRESSES (m.c.)	$3–$10
ACTORS/ACTRESSES (l.c.)	$1–$4
AMUSEMENT PARKS (e.c.)	$3–$25
Real photo	$10–$75
AMUSEMENT PARKS (m.c.)	$3–$10
AMUSEMENT PARKS (l.c.)	$2–$6
Annie Oakley (e.c.)	$3–$15
AUTO RACING (e.c.)	$10–$100
AUTO RACING (m.c.)	$2–$20
AUTO RACING (l.c.)	$1–$10
Autrey, Gene (m.c.)	$2–$10
Babe Ruth (e.c.)	$20–$50
Ball, Lucille (m.c.)	$1–$8
BASEBALL PLAYERS/TEAMS (e.c.)	$25–$500

Courtesy of John and Sandy Millns

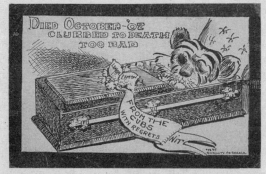

Lemons on the grave of the Tigers who "died October '07—clubbed to death—too bad—from the Cubs with regrets." The design is credited to F. P. Burke, 1907, and the postcard was published by Simplicity Co., Chicago. Rare. Value: $200.

Real photo $30–$300

Courtesy of John and Sandy Millns

Boston Red Sox, 1912 American League champions. A real photo postcard, published by Photo Art Shop. Rare. Value: $100 or more.

Courtesy of Joel Edler

The 1908 hometown baseball team from Grand Detour, Illinois. A Jurgens real photo. Scarce. Value: $15.

BASEBALL PLAYERS/TEAMS (m.c.)	$5–$35
BASEBALL PLAYERS/TEAMS (l.c.)	$2–$20
Beatles (m.c.)	$2–$20
Beatles (l.c.)	$1–$5
Bernhardt, Sarah (e.c.)	$10–$25
s/Mucha	$200–$300
BIG-BAND MUSICIANS (m.c.)	$2–$12
Billy Sunday	$5–$20
BLUES PERFORMERS (l.c.)	$1–$5

Remember! All prices in this guide represent postcards in *Excellent* condition.

BOXERS/BOXING (e.c.) $5–$20

Courtesy of John and Sandy Millns

*Advertising postcard for a boxing event at France's Luna Park.
They were promoting the December 20, 1913, world champion-
ship fight between Americans Joe Jeannette and Sam Langford.
Scarce. Value: $25 (?).*

BOXERS/BOXING (m.c.)	$3–$10
BOXERS/BOXING (l.c.)	$1–$5
Brennan, Tom (Breakfast Club, m.c.)	$2–$5
Buffalo Bill	$2–$30
CAROUSELS (e.c.)	$10–$30
Real photo	$20–$50
CAROUSELS (m.c.)	$5–$20
CAROUSELS (l.c.)	$1–$10
Chaplin, Charles (m.c.)	$2–$20
CHAUTAUQUA PERFORMERS/ADVERTISING (e.c.)	
	$5–$25
Cinerama (m.c.)	$3–$10

From the author's collection

*Chrome-finish advertising postcard for Cinerama, the cinematic
innovation of the early 1950s. Common. Value: $6.*

CIRCUS PERFORMERS/ADVERTISING (e.c.)   *$5–$30*
    Real photo   *$5–$50*

Courtesy of Joel Edler

Real photo of Millie Leatrice, a snake handler. Copyright by Campboll's Photo Art Shop, Richmond, Indiana. Rare. Value: $30.

CIRCUS PERFORMERS/ADVERTISING (m.c.)	*$2–$10*
CIRCUS PERFORMERS/ADVERTISING (l.c.)	*$1–$5*
COUNTRY/WESTERN ARTISTS (m.c.)	*$3–$25*
COUNTRY/WESTERN ARTISTS (l.c.)	*$1–$6*
DANCERS (e.c.)	*$5–$50*
DANCERS (m.c.)	*$3–$30*
DANCERS (l.c.)	*$1–$10*
Dean, James (m.c.)	*$10–$25*
Dean, James (l.c.)	*$1–$5*
Dionne quintuplets (m.c.)	*$5–$20*
Real photo	*$5–$20*
Dionne quintuplets (l.c.)	*$1–$6*
DISTANCE WALKERS (e.c.)	*$5–$20*
Evans, Dale (m.c.)	*$3–$10*
FAIRS/FESTIVALS (e.c.)	*$3–$15*
Real photo	*$5–$50*
FAIRS/FESTIVALS (m.c.)	*$2–$20*
FAIRS/FESTIVALS (l.c.)	*$1–$5*
FILM-MAKING (e.c.)	*$3–$30*
FILM-MAKING (m.c.)	*$2–$15*
FILM-MAKING (l.c.)	*$1–$5*

FOOTBALL PLAYERS/TEAMS (e.c.)	$5–$30
FOOTBALL PLAYERS/TEAMS (m.c.)	$3–$15
FOOTBALL PLAYERS/TEAMS (l.c.)	$1–$5
GAMBLING (e.c.)	$5–$50
GAMBLING (m.c.)	$2–$20

Courtesy of Joel Edler

Corey's Cafe in Las Vegas, Nevada, had two slot machines near the entrance. This early 1950s linen-style postcard was published by Beals of Des Moines, Iowa. A well-designed restaurant advertising postcard, it has a higher value because of the slot machines. Not common. Value: $15.

GAMBLING (l.c.)	$1–$5
Garbo, Greta (m.c.)	$10–$25
Garbo, Greta (l.c.)	$1–$5
GOLF (e.c.)	$3–$20
GOLF (m.c.)	$2–$15
GOLF (l.c.)	$1–$5
Grateful Dead (l.c.)	$1–$5

The minimum value in this price guide is $1. While many dealers offer 25-cent and 50-cent "bargain boxes," few dealers sort, individually price, and protectively "sleeve" postcards valued at less than $1. This price guide offers values for postcards worth $1 or more.

HORSE RACING (e.c.) $5–$75

SOUVENIR
The Great Allentown Fair, Allentown, Pa.
SEPTEMBER 18-21, 1906

DAN PATCH

RECORD: 1:55 MILE TRACK; 2:01 HALF-MILE TRACK

Dan Patch, winning race horse, is featured on this souvenir post-card from the Allentown, Pennsylvania, fair of 1906. A rare undivided-back postcard. Value: $75. (More common Dan Patch postcards sell for $40–$50.)

HORSE RACING (m.c.)	$2–$25
HORSE RACING (l.c.)	$1–$5
HOTELS/ADVERTISING (pio.)	$20–$50
HOTELS/ADVERTISING (e.c.)	$3–$15
HOTELS/ADVERTISING (m.c.)	$1–$10
HOTELS/ADVERTISING (l.c.)	$1–$2
ICE SKATERS/SPORTS (e.c.)	$3–$30
ICE SKATERS/SPORTS (m.c.)	$2–$20
ICE SKATERS/SPORTS (l.c.)	$1–$5

JAZZ PERFORMERS (m.c.) $2–$20

From the author's collection

A World War II-era advertising postcard issued by RCA Victor, one of a series of eighteen of jazz and big-band recording artists. The Lena Horne card is one of three featuring female performers. Not common. Value: $12.

JAZZ PERFORMERS (l.c.)	$1–$5
LINCOLN HIGHWAY (m.c.)	$2–$8
Lone Ranger (m.c.)	$2–$12

Courtesy of Joel Edler

Children's cowboy hero, the Lone Ranger, was featured on this advertising postcard issued by General Mills of Minneapolis. The action painting, copyright T.L.R., Inc., includes a facsimile autograph. Not common. Value: $6.

Marx Brothers (m.c.)	$6–$8
Marx Brothers (l.c.)	$1–$2

MINIATURE GOLF (m.c.)	$2–$15
MINIATURE GOLF (l.c.)	$1–$6
Monroe, Marilyn (m.c.)	$5–$20
Real photo	$5–$20

Courtesy of *Postcard Collector*

Marilyn Monroe on a standard-size postcard from early in her career. Common. Value: $4.

Monroe, Marilyn (l.c.)	$1–$5
MOTELS/ADVERTISING (m.c.)	$2–$20
MOTELS/ADVERTISING (l.c.)	$1–$5
MOVIE STARS/HOMES (e.c.)	$2–$10
MOVIE STARS/HOMES (m.c.)	$1–$6
MOVIE STARS/HOMES (l.c.)	$1–$3
MOXIE	$20–$120
Nesbit, Evelyn (e.c.)	$5–$15

Courtesy of *Postcard Collector*

Early-century actress Evelyn Nesbit posing with tiger head. Black and white divided-back postcard. Not common. Value: $12.

OPERA (e.c.)	$5–$40
OPERA (m.c.)	$3–$20
OPERA (l.c.)	$1–$5
Owens, Jesse (m.c.)	$20–$60

Courtesy of John and Sandy Millns

1936 real photo postcard of athlete Jesse Owens. Scarce. Value:
$50.

PARADES (e.c.)	$3–$20
Real photo	$5–$35
PARADES (m.c.)	$2–$10
PARADES (l.c.)	$1–$5
Paul Bunyan (m.c.)	$2–$8
Paul Bunyan (l.c.)	$1–$3
PENNSYLVANIA TURNPIKE (m.c.)	$1–$3
Pickford, Mary (e.c.)	$3–$15
Presley, Elvis (m.c.)	$5–$15
Presley, Elvis (l.c.)	$1–$3
Quiz Kids (m.c.)	$8–$10

From the author's collection

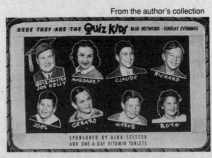

*Quiz Kids radio show, sponsored by Alka-Seltzer. Listeners send-
ing in questions received the postcards as acknowledgment. Not
common.* Value: $10.

RADIO STARS/ADVERTISING (e.c.)	$5–$15
RADIO STARS/ADVERTISING (m.c.)	$2–$10
RADIO STARS/ADVERTISING (l.c.)	$1–$3
RECORDING ARTISTS (e.c.)	$5–$20
RECORDING ARTISTS (m.c.)	$2–$20
RECORDING ARTISTS (l.c.)	$1–$5
RESTAURANTS/ADVERTISING (e.c.)	$3–$10
RESTAURANTS/ADVERTISING (m.c.)	$1–$10
RESTAURANTS/ADVERTISING (l.c.)	$1–$3
ROADSIDE ATTRACTIONS (e.c.)	$5–$30
Real photo	$5–$40
ROADSIDE ATTRACTIONS (m.c.)	$3–$20

From the author's collection

VINELAND, NEW JERSEY, U.S.A

George Daynor — Originator, Designer and Builder

The Palace of Depression in Vineland, New Jersey; a nice example of a roadside attraction on a linen-finish postcard, ca. 1930s. Not common. Value: $12.

ROADSIDE ATTRACTIONS (l.c.)	$1–$5
ROCK & ROLL PERFORMERS/ADVERTISING (l.c.)	
	$1–$20
RODEO PERFORMERS (e.c.)	$3–$10
Real photo	$5–$20
RODEO PERFORMERS (m.c.)	$2–$10
RODEO PERFORMERS (l.c.)	$1–$3
Rogers, Roy (m.c.)	$2–$6
ROUTE 66 (m.c.)	$2–$8
ROUTE 66 (l.c.)	$1–$3
STARS 'N' STRIPES (e.c.)	$3–$20
Real photo	$5–$50
STARS 'N' STRIPES (m.c.)	$1–$15
STARS 'N' STRIPES (l.c.)	$1–$3

STATUE OF LIBERTY (e.c.)	$3–$20
STATUE OF LIBERTY (m.c.)	$1–$5
STATUE OF LIBERTY (l.c.)	$1–$2
Stilt walkers (e.c.)	$10–$30
TELEVISION PERFORMERS (m.c.)	$3–$15
TELEVISION PERFORMERS (l.c.)	$1–$5
Temple, Shirley (m.c.)	$10–$30
Temple, Shirley (l.c.)	$1–$3
UNCLE SAM (e.c.)	$5–$25
Real photo	$15–$100
UNCLE SAM (m.c.)	$3–$15
UNCLE SAM (l.c.)	$1–$5
VAUDEVILLE/MUSIC HALL PERFORMERS (e.c.)	
	$5–$25
WATER SPORTS (e.c.)	$3–$20
WATER SPORTS (m.c.)	$2–$10
WATER SPORTS (l.c.)	$1–$3
Wayne, John (l.c.)	$1–$4
Wild West shows (e.c.)	$5–$50
WINTER SPORTS (e.c.)	$3–$30
WINTER SPORTS (m.c.)	$2–$10
WINTER SPORTS (l.c.)	$1–$3
ZOOS (e.c.)	$2–$5
ZOOS (m.c.)	$1–$2
ZOOS (l.c.)	$1–$2

EXPOSITIONS, FAIRS, AND DATED EVENTS

Supply is greater than demand for most exposition postcards—
from the pioneers to the present! Prices are relatively low except
for rare items.

Of the American pioneer expo issues, some from the 1893 Columbian Exposition are much more common than those from
events which occurred later in the decade.

Advertising postcards given away by expo exhibitors have survived in much smaller quantities than the official issues. This
relative rarity, combined with more interesting subject matter,
makes most ad cards more valuable.

Local events commemorated on postcards are most often collected for their regional interest. Demand can be as erratic as for view cards of any specific location.

Expo postcards mailed at the event with appropriate stamp and cancellation may be valued much higher than unused postcards. The values in these listings represent unused postcards in Excellent condition. The value of used postcards may depend on the value of the stamp; this information can be found in a stamp catalog. In this section, the listings also appear in chronological order.

EXPOSITIONS, FAIRS, AND DATED EVENTS VALUES

1893 WORLD'S COLUMBIAN EXPOSITION

	$12–$800
Anonymous publishers	*$100–$800*
p/Goldsmith (pre-off)	*$100–$150*
p/Goldsmith (off, ser 1, 10 des)	*$12–$15*
p/Goldsmith (off, ser 1, 12 des)	*$15–$18*
p/Koehler, postal card back	*$40–$50*
Other advertising	*$100–$175*
Puck advertising	*$150*
R. Selinger designs	*$125–$150*

Official issue for the World's Columbian Exposition published by Goldsmith, Series 1, design 9. Value: $15.

From the author's collection

Unofficial issue published by Jos. Koehler. Scarce. Value: $45.

From the author's collection

Columbian Exposition unofficial issue, a line drawing by Selinger. Rare. Value: $125–$150.

1894 CALIFORNIA MIDWINTER	$125–$180
p/Hergert (off)	$125–$150
"Official Souvenir" (4 cards)	$150–$180
"Souvenir" (5 cards)	$150–$180

Courtesy of *Postcard Collector*

"Official Souvenir Correspondence Card" for the California Midwinter International Exposition, San Francisco, 1894. This card shows the Electric Tower and the Fine and Decorative Arts Building. Rare. Value: $150.

1895 COTTON STATES p/Baum (off) $140–$150

Courtesy of *Postcard Collector*

Official souvenir postcard for the Cotton States and International Exposition, the Minerals and Forestry Building. Rare. Value: $140–$150.

1897 TENNESSEE CENTENNIAL	$180–$200
1898 TRANS-MISSISSIPPI	$35–$125
p/Albertype	$100–$125
Fleischmann ad	$75–$100
Official (on postal card)	$35–$45

Courtesy of *Postcard Collector*

Rare advertising postcard available at Fleischmann's Yeast booth at the Trans-Mississippi Exposition and International Exposition, also known as the Omaha Exposition, 1898. Value: $100.

1898 WORCESTER SEMI-CENTENNIAL	$80–$100
1900 PARIS EXPOSITION	$10–$350
1900: June 30 HOBOKEN (NJ) PIER FIRE	$8–$20

1901 PAN-AMERICAN EXPOSITION $5–$100
    Advertising issues $5–$50
    p/Niagra Envelope (off, b/w) $7–$8
    p/Niagra Envelope (off, color) $8–$9
    p/Niagra Envelope (off, oversize)
                            $90–$100
    p/Niagra Envelope (off, amusements)
                            $15–$18
    Unofficial publishers $8–$80

Courtesy of *Postcard Collector*

Scarce stamp postcard issued by F. A. Busch for the Pan-American Exposition, Buffalo, 1901. Value: $50.

1902 SOUTH CAROLINA INTERSTATE $75–$125
    p/Albertype (off) $75–$100
    Unofficial issues $100–$125

Courtesy of *Postcard Collector*

An example from the official private mailing cards published by the Albertype Co. of Brooklyn, New York, for the South Carolina Interstate and West Indian Exposition, Charleston. Value: $75–$100.

1904 LOUISIANA PURCHASE EXPOSITION (ST. LOUIS)

	$5–$100
p/Adams	*$9–$10*
p/Buxton & Skinner	*$10–$12*
p/Chisholm	*$5–$6*
Cook advertising	*$9–$10*
p/Cupples (off)	*$5–$7*
p/Cupples (pebble)	*$6–$8*
p/Cupples (silver "transparency")	*$6–$8*
p/Cupples (hold-to-light)	*$30–$40*
p/Frey	*$5–$6*
p/Hammon	*$6–$7*
p/Hesse	*$9–$10*
Hold-to-light Inside Inn	*$100*
Hold-to-light (6 × 9 inches, 5 diff)	*$300*
p/Illustrated Postal Card (woven silk)	
	$100–$200
p/Jordan	*$4–$5*
p/Koehler	*$4–$5*
p/Kropp	*$4–$5*
p/McFarlane	*$5–$6*
p/Mogul Cigarettes ads	*$10–$12*
Peter advertising	*$9–$10*
p/Pinkau	*$8–$10*
p/Post Dispatch	*$6–$7*
Regal advertising	*$6–$7*
p/Rosenblatt	*$20–$25*
p/Rotograph	*$5–$6*
p/Selige	*$6–$7*
Singer advertising	*$7–$8*
p/Tuck	*$8–$15*

Remember! All prices in this guide represent postcards in *Excellent* condition.

Wood, metal, and novelty cards   *$5–$15*

Official souvenir postcard, pebble surface, published by the Samuel Cupples Envelope Co. of St. Louis-New York, the "sole stationery licensee" for the 1904 St. Louis Expo. Common. Value: $8.

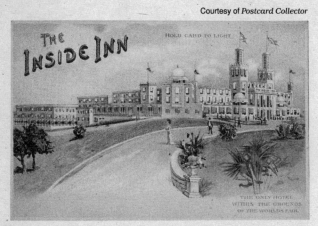

The Inside Inn, the rarest and most valuable of the hold-to-light series published by Samuel Cupples Envelope Co. Value: $100.

1905 LEWIS & CLARK EXPOSITION	*$8–$15*
Advertising	*$8–$10*
p/Charlton	*$8–$10*
p/Gill	*$8–$10*
p/Mitchell	*$8–$10*
p/Pinkau	*$12–$15*
p/B. B. Rich (off, silver)	*$12–$15*

p/Selige   *$8–$10*

Agricultural Palace at the Lewis & Clark Exposition, Portland, Oregon, 1905, by an anonymous publisher. Value: $10.

1906: April 18 SAN FRANCISCO EARTHQUAKE
                                   $3–$15
1907 JAMESTOWN EXPOSITION   *$5–$75*
    Advertising   *$5–$25*
    p/Bosselman   *$8–$10*
    p/Illustrated Postcard (embossed)
                                   $40–$50
    p/Jamestown A & V (off, 185 diff)
                                   $12–$15
    p/Jamestown A & V (off, warships)
                                   $15–$30
    p/Jamestown A & V, #60, #61   *$60–$70*
    p/Jamestown A & V, s/Christy, army/navy
    girls   *$75*
    Teddy bear moving picture mailing card
                                   $500(?)

"The Handclasp of Centuries" shows Theodore Roosevelt and his "De-e-lighted. . . .!" Not common. Value: $15.

p/Tuck (silvers, 8 diff)	$15–$18
p/Tuck (Oilette)	$10–$12
p/Tuck (photochrome)	$8–$10
p/Tuck (three-panel)	$40–$50
1907–09 PRIESTS OF PALLAS	$15–$18
1908 PHILADELPHIA FOUNDERS WEEK	$8–$10
p/Illustrated Postcard, ser 254 (10 diff)	
	$8–$10
p/Lounsbury (10 diff)	$8–$10
1908 APPALACHIAN EXPOSITION (KNOXVILLE)	$5
1908 OHIO STATE FAIR (COLUMBUS)	$5
1909 ALASKA YUKON-PACIFIC EXPOSITION	$3–$10
Advertising	$5–$10
p/Edward H. Mitchell	$4–$6
p/Portland Postcard (200+ diff, off)	
	$3–$5
p/Reid	$4–$5
1909 HUDSON-FULTON CELEBRATION	$4–$10
p/Churchman	$4–$6
p/Koehler: Par Excellence ser (6 diff)	
	$6–$8
p/Lounsbury	$8–$10
p/Redfield: Float set (72 diff)	$7–$8
p/Remick	$6–$8
p/Rose	$6–$8
p/Tuck, ser 164	$8–$10
p/Valentine, Uncle Sam, s/Wall	$7
1909 RICHMOND, INDIANA, FALL FESTIVAL	$4
1909 PORTOLA FESTIVAL	$4–$12

Remember! All prices in this guide represent postcards in *Excellent* condition.

1911 MINNEAPOLIS CIVIC CELEBRATION   *$8–$12*

Courtesy of *Postcard Collector*

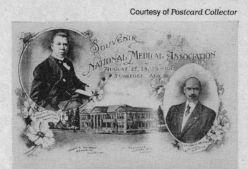

Souvenir of the National Medical Association, August 27–29, 1912, shows Booker T. Washington and Dr. John A. Kenney, Tuskegee, Alabama. Rare. Value: $25.

1913 STATE FAIR OF TEXAS (DALLAS)   *$5*
1915 PANAMA-PACIFIC EXPOSITION   *$3–$8*
  p/Behrendt (Taft and Uncle Sam, pre-issue)   *$25*

Courtesy of *Postcard Collector*

"The California Sandwich" hypes both the Panama-Pacific in San Francisco and the Panama-California in San Diego while making sure the viewer is aware that Los Angeles is between the two locales. Value: $25.

A Panama-Pacific pre-issue, copyright 1911 by Richard Behrendt, shows Uncle Sam being welcomed back to San Francisco. Cliff House is shown in the background. Not common. Value: $25.

1915 PANAMA-CALIFORNIA	$3–$8
Pre-expo issues	$6–$12
1915: July 24 SINKING OF EASTLAKE, CHICAGO	$6–$10

"The Friends of Peace" postcard was an invitation to a Labor Day National Peace Convention in Chicago, 1915. The printed silk flag ripples over a wax matrix. Not common. Value: $30.

1933–34 CENTURY OF PROGRESS (CHICAGO)   *$1–$8*
     Advertising   *$3–$8*
     Comics   *$4–$6*
     Exhibit buildings   *$1–$3*

From the author's collection

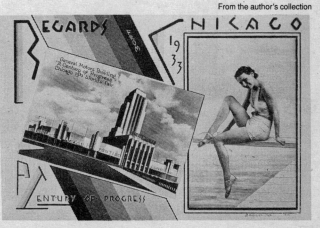

Unofficial 1933 Century of Progress photo postcard combines a view, Art Deco graphics, and a pinup. Not common. Value: $8.

1936 TEXAS CENTENNIAL   *$1–$8*

The minimum value in this price guide is $1. While many dealers offer 25-cent and 50-cent "bargain boxes," few dealers sort, individually price, and protectively "sleeve" postcards valued at less than $1. This price guide offers values for postcards worth $1 or more.

1939 NEW YORK WORLD'S FAIR $1–$8

From the author's collection

1939 New York World's Fair Trylon and Perisphere. Printed in gold, orange, and indigo on undersize (3⅛ × 5 inches) stock. Common. Value: $4

Courtesy of John and Sandy Millns

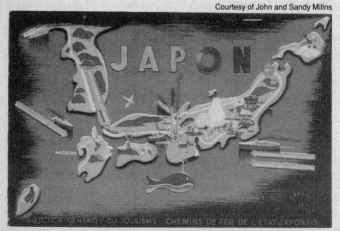

Rare postcard intended for the 1940 Olympics in Japan. Value: $40.

1962 SEATTLE WORLD'S FAIR $1–$6

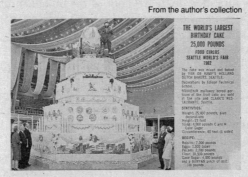

From the author's collection

World's largest birthday cake—25,000 pounds with Paul Bunyan on the top (his 128th birthday)—was displayed at the 1962 Seattle World's Fair, courtesy of Clark's Restaurant Enterprises. The postcard promoted cane sugar. Not common. Value: $6.

1964–65 NEW YORK WORLD'S FAIR $1–$5
1984 OLYMPIC GAMES, LOS ANGELES $1–$3

From the author's collection

1984 Olympics maximum card from the series of sixteen cards issued by the U.S. Postal Service, advertising and commemorating the 1984 Olympics. The picture reproduces the design on one of the 13-cent postage stamps. The July 28, 1983, postmark is a "first-day" cancellation. Value: $3.

1984 LOUISIANA WORLD EXPOSITION $1–$2

FAMILY, PEOPLE, AND EVERYDAY LIFE

This section includes postcards about the objects and activities of everyday people and everyday life—at home, at work, and at play. These include both postcards produced from photographs as well as artist-drawn postcards.

Early real photo postcards of anonymous people reveal the behavior, fashions, and paraphernalia of work, family, and social life. Unusual items can still be found because many were made by amateur photographers and never left the family. One-of-a-kind real photos as examples of early 20th-century Americana are avidly sought.

Mass-produced postcards also show many facets and paraphernalia of everyday life from birth through marriage to death. The approach may be humorous or sentimental, or the design may feature an ad pitching a product hoped to be essential to every home. These everyday postcards may also reveal everyday people's attitudes toward other ethnic or religious groups, toward patriotism, and toward proper behavior.

FAMILY, PEOPLE, AND EVERYDAY LIFE VALUES

THE WATER WAGON WOULD SEEM TO BE OVERDUE

He's fat, he smokes, and he drinks to excess. All three facets of anti-social behavior are humorously portrayed on the card, but the emphasis is clearly on alcoholism/temperance. A scarce postcard. Value: $6.

AMISH (e.c.)	*$10–$30*
AMISH (m.c.)	*$3–$15*
AMISH (l.c.)	*$1–$3*
BABIES (e.c.)	*$3–$20*

From the author's collection

Four babies in yellow dresses carry a flag supporting "Votes for Our Mothers." Artist-signed O'Neill and copyright 1915 by the National Woman Suffrage Publishing Co. This is the rarest O'Neill suffrage card. Value: $300.

Real photo	*$1–$8*
BABIES (m.c.)	*$1–$5*
BABIES (l.c.)	*$1–$2*
BIRTH (e.c.)	*$3–$15*
BIRTH (m.c.)	*$1–$8*
BIRTH (l.c.)	*$1–$3*

Remember! All prices in this guide represent postcards in *Excellent* condition.

BLACKS (pio.)	$25–$35
p/Albertype	$25–$35
p/Livingston	$25–$35
BLACKS (e.c.)	$5–$30

Courtesy of Fred Schiffman

A private mailing card published by Arthur Livingston of New York. It is card #26, "Way Down South in Dixie," portraying blacks in a social setting. Not common. Value: $10. (The identical Livingston design on a pioneer—before 1898—postcard would be valued at $30.)

Real photo	$8–$40
p/Tuck	$8–$25
BLACKS (m.c.)	$5–$20
BLACKS (l.c.)	$1–$3

The minimum value in this price guide is $1. While many dealers offer 25-cent and 50-cent "bargain boxes," few dealers sort, individually price, and protectively "sleeve" postcards valued at less than $1. This price guide offers values for postcards worth $1 or more.

| CHILDREN (e.c.) | $2–$25 |
| p/PFB | $5–$20 |

A sentimental artist-drawn (unsigned) interpretation of children at play. An embossed postcard published by PFB (Paul Finkenrath, Berlin). Not common. Value: $15.

Real photo	$3–$30
p/Tuck	$3–$15
CHILDREN (m.c.)	$1–$10
CHILDREN (l.c.)	$1–$3
COLLEGE LIFE (e.c.)	$6–$30

Dance class at West Point. Raphael Tuck & Sons, series 2322, "Life at West Point." Copyright by Waldon Fawcett, an undivided-back postcard, postally used in August 1906. Common. Value: $8.

Real photo	$5–$50
COLLEGE LIFE (m.c.)	$2–$10
COLLEGE LIFE (l.c.)	$1–$3

COURTSHIP (e.c.)	$3–$15
p/Bamforth	$3–$10
s/Fisher	$10–$15
COURTSHIP (m.c.)	$1–$3
COURTSHIP (l.c.)	$1–$2
DEATH (e.c.)	$5–$30

Courtesy of *Postcard Collector*

Death and sentiments of sympathy are uncommon on postcards. A divided-back postcard. Value: $20.

Real photo	$3–$40
DEATH (m.c.)	$2–$15
DEATH (l.c.)	$1–$3
FAMILY ENTERTAINMENTS (e.c.)	$3–$30
Real photo	$5–$75

From the author's collection

Five young women wearing special dresses that form a flag design when they stand close together. A rare real photo. Value: $50.

FAMILY ENTERTAINMENTS (m.c.)	$2–$15

FAMILY ENTERTAINMENTS (l.c.)	$1–$10
FASHIONS, MEN'S (e.c.)	$5–$30
Real photo	$3–$20
FASHIONS, MEN'S (m.c.)	$2–$20
FASHIONS, MEN'S (l.c.)	$1–$3
FASHIONS, WOMEN'S (e.c.)	$5–$40
Real photo	$3–$30
FASHIONS, WOMEN'S (m.c.)	$3–$20
FASHIONS, WOMEN'S (l.c.)	$1–$3
FOOD (e.c.)	$3–$30
Real photo	$3–$20
FOOD (m.c.)	$2–$20
FOOD (l.c.)	$1–$5
FRATERNAL ORGANIZATIONS (e.c.)	$5–$30
Real photo	$5–$60
FRATERNAL ORGANIZATIONS (m.c.)	$2–$15
FRATERNAL ORGANIZATIONS (l.c.)	$1–$5
GAMES AND TOYS (e.c.)	$5–$250
Real photo	$5–$100
GAMES AND TOYS (m.c.)	$3–$30
Queen's Doll House, p/Tuck	$8–$10
Titania's Palace, p/Tuck	$8–$10
GAMES AND TOYS (l.c.)	$1–$5
p/Ackert	$1–$3
HOME (e.c.)	$3–$30
Real photo	$3–$30

From the author's collection

"Mollie and I and The Babies." A sod house with a windowed door.
Real photo postcard with Solomon D. Butcher credit on the back.
Scarce. Value: $15.

Courtesy of *Postcard Collector*

Real photo of an early "mobile home"—a one-log cabin, a Douglas fir log hauled on a Dodge Bros. three-ton truck. Scarce. Value: $20.

HOME (m.c.)	$2–$20
HOME (l.c.)	$1–$3
HOME APPLIANCES (e.c.)	$3–$30
HOME APPLIANCES (m.c.)	$2–$20
HOME APPLIANCES (l.c.)	$1–$5
HOME FURNISHINGS (e.c.)	$3–$25
Real photo	$3–$30
HOME FURNISHINGS (m.c.)	$2–$15
HOME FURNISHINGS (l.c.)	$1–$10
HOMETOWN EVENTS (e.c.)	$5–$100

From the author's collection

A rare real photo of Uncle Sam on stilts carrying an advertising sandwich board. Adding interest to the action photo is the community band. The three-story apartment buildings in the background indicate that the setting is urban, not small-town. Value: $80.

HOMETOWN EVENTS (m.c.)	$2–$20
HOMETOWN EVENTS (l.c.)	$1–$6

House of David	$8–$20
INDIANS (pio.)	$25–$35
p/Livingston	$25–$35
INDIANS (e.c.)	$3–$25
Real photo	$5–$40
INDIANS (m.c.)	$2–$6
INDIANS (l.c.)	$1–$3
JUDAICA	$8–$100
JUDAICA	$3–$20
JUDAICA	$1–$8
MARRIAGE (e.c.)	$3–$20
Real photo	$3–$20
MARRIAGE (m.c.)	$2–$8
s/Hatlo	$5–$6
MARRIAGE (l.c.)	$1–$3
MILITARY LIFE (e.c.)	$3–$20
MILITARY LIFE (m.c.)	$3–$10
s/Breger	$6–$8
MILITARY LIFE (l.c.)	$1–$5
SCHOOL (e.c.)	$3–$35
Real photo	$5–$35
SCHOOL (m.c.)	$2–$12
SCHOOL (l.c.)	$1–$3
SCOUTING (e.c.)	$10–$40
Real photo	$5–$30
SCOUTING (m.c.)	$2–$15
SCOUTING (l.c.)	$1–$3
"Scouts of the World"	$1–$2
SOCIAL ACTIVITIES (e.c.)	$5–$50

Courtesy of Fred Schiffman

Real photo of a pool hall. An Oxley photo. Scarce. Value: $35.

SOCIAL ACTIVITIES (m.c.) $2–$25

Courtesy of Postcard Collector

Linen-period dance action. From a 10-card series, "C.T. Jitterbug Comics," published in 1938 by Curt Teich. Rare. Value: $25.

SOCIAL ACTIVITIES (l.c.)   *$1–$5*
SPORTS (e.c.)   *$3–$50*
Real photo   *$5–$50*

Courtesy of Joel Edler

Real photo view of the Viking Ski Club of Arbor Vitae, Wisconsin, taken at the foot of the ski jump. It appears to be a ceremonial photo preceding a funeral. Note the flag-draped coffin halfway up the hill. Photo by G. A. Lau. Rare. Value: $15.

SPORTS (m.c.)   *$2–$10*
SPORTS (l.c.)   *$1–$5*
SUNBONNET BABIES (e.c.)   *$5–$20*
SUNBONNET BABIES (l.c. reproductions)   *$1–$3*

WOMEN'S ORGANIZATIONS (e.c.)	$3–$25
Real photo	$3–$25
WOMEN'S ORGANIZATIONS (m.c.)	$2–$15
WOMEN'S ORGANIZATIONS (l.c.)	$1–$5
WORKING (e.c.)	$3–$50
Cries of London	$10–$12
Cries of Paris	$12–$15
Real photo	$8–$80

Courtesy of Joel Edler

Four telephone operators and their supervisor. This is a superb real photo: a detail-filled interior view of pre–World War I working women. Published by A. J. Kingsbury of Antigo, Wisconsin, postally used 1908. Rare. Value: $50.

Courtesy of Joel Edler

Boldigs Mill and its crew of Norway, Wisconsin, stopped work for this outdoor portrait. Pre–World War I, divided-back real photo postcard, a C. J. Ruppenthal photo. Scarce. Value: $20.

WORKING (m.c.) $2–$20

PART OF THE UNDERWRITING, ENDORSEMENT AND PRODUCTION DEPARTMENTS

NATIONAL GRANGE MUTUAL LIABILITY AND FIRE INSURANCE COMPANIES KEENE, NEW HAMPSHIRE

Women office workers, probably 1930s. This linen-finish interior view shows part of the underwriting, endorsement, and production departments at the National Grange Mutual Liability and Fire Insurance Co. of Keene, New Hampshire. Not common. Value: $12.

WORKING (l.c.) $1–$10

FANTASY, GLAMOUR, AND EROTICA

This section includes postcards showing the creatures and characters of fantasy and fiction; people and animals transformed by fantasy; glamour and erotica; and humor and other works of the imagination.

Artist-drawn fantasy postcards were produced in much greater numbers during the early part of the century than any time since. They are avidly collected today.

Dressed animals find a wide collecting audience, and glamour and erotica postcards of all decades find eager buyers. European metamorphic cards command high prices, as do American photo montage postcards. The latter are eagerly collected and there is great competition for rare ones.

Contemporary Disney postcards are produced in very large numbers and enjoy a very wide audience. Some early Disney (especially Mickey Mouse) postcards as well as early Disneyland postcards support high prices.

Postcards of Garfield the cat, universally popular in the 1980s, are widely collected, as is Gary Larsen's "The Far Side" series.

Some of the finest quality printing on postcards, e.g. Stengle and Sborgi, occurs in the fine art category. Museum reproductions have long enjoyed wide appreciation by the public and a wealth of material exists. However, little of it—with the exception of female nudes—has much appeal with collectors.

FANTASY, GLAMOUR, AND EROTICA VALUES

Alice in Wonderland (e.c.) $8–$30

From the author's collection

Alice in Wonderland, one of a series drawn by artist C. M. Burd for Fralinger's Salt Water Taffy ads. Note the boxes of taffy falling off the trees. A desirable pre–World War I series. Scarce. Value: $30.

BATHING BEAUTIES (e.c.)	$5–$30
s/H. King	$10–$15
BATHING BEAUTIES (m.c.)	$4–$15
BATHING BEAUTIES (l.c.)	$1–$2
Batman (l.c.)	$1–$4
BUSTER BROWN (e.c.)	$8–$30
Busy Bears p/Austen	$10–$15
Cabbage Patch Babies (e.c.)	$6–$12

COLLEGE GIRLS (e.c.)	$8–$70
s/F. Earl Christy	$10–$20
"College Kings" ser 2766, p/Tuck	
	$60–$70
"College Queens" ser 2767, p/Tuck	
	$60–$70
p/Ullman	$8–$12
University Girls, p/Tuck	$10–$20
Crackerjack Bears (e.c.)	$25–$30
DICKENS (e.c.)	$8–$15
In Dickens Land Series	$8–$10

Courtesy of *Postcard Collector*

From the Tuck sets "In Dickens Land." A desirable series. Scarce. Value: $10.

s/KYD	$15–$18
DISNEY (m.c.)	$2–$20
DISNEY (l.c.)	$1–$3
DISNEY-EPCOT	$1–$3

Remember! All prices in this guide represent postcards in *Excellent* condition.

DISNEYLAND (m.c.) $2–$250

Courtesy of *Postcard Collector*

A rare black and white real photo postcard of Sleeping Beauty's Castle at Disneyland. This early postcard was available on the racks at Disneyland for a very short time. Value: $250.

DISNEYLAND (l.c.)	$1–$3
DISNEYWORLD (l.c.)	$1–$3
DRESSED BEARS (e.c.)	$8–$30
Busy Bears, p/Austen	$10–$15
Cavally Bears, p/Thayer	$15–$20
s/Rose Clark, p/Rotograph	$15–$18
Crackerjack Bears	$25–$30
p/Heal	$10–$12
s/Fritz Hildebrandt, p/Tuck	$20–$25
p/Ottmann	$6–$8
Roosevelt Bears	$15–$75
p/Tower M & N	$7–$10
s/Wall, p/Ullman, days of week	$10–$15
DRESSED CATS	$1–$250
p/Mainzer (m.c.)	$1–$5
s/Wain (e.c.)	$30–$250
DRESSED DOGS (e.c.)	$8–$20
DRESSED FROGS (e.c.)	$8–$25
DRESSED PIGS (e.c.)	$5–$35
ELVES (e.c.)	$5–$25
ELVES (m.c.)	$1–$10
ELVES (l.c.)	$1–$2

EROTIC (e.c.)	$15–$30
Real photo	$20–$30
EROTIC (m.c.)	$10–$20
EROTIC (l.c.)	$1–$10
EXAGGERATED FRUIT (e.c.), p/Mitchell	$1–$4
EXAGGERATED HATS (e.c.), p/Acme	$6–$10
EXAGGERATION (e.c.)	$5–$75
p/Colby	$3–$6
p/Conard	$10–$20
Frogs	$100
s/W. H.Martin	$8–$100
EXAGGERATION (m.c.)	$1–$15

Courtesy of Fred Schiffman

Linen-style exaggeration. Published in 1946 by Curt Teich & Co.
Common. Value: $4.

EXAGGERATION (l.c.)	$1–$3
FAIRY TALES (e.c.)	$5–$35
s/Lorna Steele	$8–$10
FAIRY TALES (m.c.)	$1–$8
FAIRY TALES (l.c.)	$1–$2
Far Side s/Larsen (l.c.)	$1–$2
FUTURISM	$2–$50
Garfield s/Davis (l.c.)	$1–$2
Issued outside U.S.	$3–$5

GLAMOUR (e.c.) $10–$400

Courtesy of Fred Schiffman

Art Nouveau, artist-signed Gaston Noury. Design is highlighted with intricate decorative detail and subtle shading on the face. The darkened eyes, flowing veil, and vapors wafting from the flacons all add mystery and an erotic aura. Pre–World War I, divided back. Rare. Value: $100.

GLAMOUR (m.c.) $3–$20

From the author's collection

There was less mystery on mid-century glamour. A linen-finish postcard. Common. Value: $5.

GLAMOUR (l.c.)	$1–$2
GOLLIWOGS	$10–$40
s/Florence Upton	$30–$40
Gone with the Wind (l.c.)	$1–$3

Guinnipens, s/G. M. Hudson, p/Tuck

	$12–$15
Hiawatha	$1–$10
HUMOR (e.c.)	$1–$15

Humor can go out of style rapidly. What's funny to one generation or in one decade may be impenetrable to the next. The "Darnphool Questions" were a popular postcard series in the early divided-back period. Some cards are artist-signed Wall. Orange and black on white. Not common. Value: $8.

HUMOR (m.c.)	$1–$8
HUMOR (l.c.)	$1–$2
Jiggs and Maggi, s/Geo. McManus	$20–$40
KEWPIES s/O'Neill	$35–$60
Little Nemo (p/Tuck)	$25–$30

Winsor McCay's twelve "Little Nemo" postcard designs are scarce but desirable. Copyright 1907 by the New York Herald, published by Raphael Tuck & Sons. This design of Nemo and friends, dwarfed by giant skyscrapers, is considered the most surreal. Value: $30.

Lovely Lilly, s/G. F. Kaber, p/Lounsbury
$45–$50
LOVERS/ROMANCE (e.c.) $3–$15
LOVERS/ROMANCE (m.c.) $1–$4
LOVERS/ROMANCE (l.c.) $1–$2
Men of Letters Series, p/Tuck, s/C. W. Quinnell
$12–$15
METAMORPHIC (e.c.) $30–$60

Courtesy of Postcard Collector

A PFB photomontage of a satyr and four nude women with cocktail glasses which, when looked at from a different angle, changes into a beak-nosed, bearded man. An unusual fantasy subject. Scarce. Value: $40.

MICKEY MOUSE (m.c.) $3–$30

Courtesy of Postcard Collector

SORRY, I CAN'T GET AWAY TO SEE YOU!

An early Mickey Mouse. Not common. Value: $12.

MICKEY MOUSE (l.c.)	$1–$5
MONTAGE (e.c.)	$5–$50

From the author's collection

A giant chicken pulling a wagon of giant eggs is representative of early-century photomontage postcards. Other subjects included hares, cornstalks, and farm products. Not common. Value: $12.

NATIONAL GIRLS	$8–$15
p/National Art	$8–$12
p/Platinachrome	$10–$15
NUDES (e.c.)	$15–$30
Real photo	$20–$30
NUDES (m.c.)	$10–$20
NUDES (l.c.)	$1–$10
NURSERY RHYMES (e.c.)	$3–$30
p/Fralinger's Taffy, s/Burd	$25–$30
NURSERY RHYMES (m.c.)	$2–$15
p/Medici Society	$6–$8
p/Warne, Randolph Caldecott art	
	$6–$10
NURSERY RHYMES (l.c.)	$1–$4
p/Medici Society	$1

👈

The minimum value in this price guide is $1. While many dealers offer 25-cent and 50-cent "bargain boxes," few dealers sort, individually price, and protectively "sleeve" postcards valued at less than $1. This price guide offers values for postcards worth $1 or more.

PAUL BUNYAN (m.c.)	$3–$8
PAUL BUNYAN (l.c.)	$1–$3
Piggie Wiggie, p/Tuck	$25–$35
Pop-eye (l.c.)	$1–$8
Postcard "storiettes" (m.c.)	$6

From the author's collection

A linen-finish postcard published in 1943 by Lollesgard, this is #3 of a series of eighteen western "storiettes." A desirable group. Not common. Value: $6.

Quaddy (e.c.) $20–$25

Courtesy of Postcard Collector

Danny Meadow Mouse, one of ten characters drawn by Harrison Cady (signed H. Cady), copyrighted and licensed by Thornton Burgess for Quaddy Playthings Mfg. Co. of Kansas City, Missouri. A desirable set of postcards. Scarce. Value: $25.

Queen's Doll House, p/Tuck $8–$10

Roosevelt bears, c/Edw. Stern, #1–16

	$15–$20
No. 17–32	$25–$35
Uncle Sam	$30–$40
Un-numbered	$50–$75

Courtesy of Joel Edler

No. 20 from the second series of Roosevelt bears. Scarce. Value:
$20.

Sambo (l.c.) $2

From the author's collection

Sambo's Picture Story Cards

8 Different Post Cards

*Windowed envelope with postcards inside. Eight postcards adver-
tising Sambo's Restaurants, 1960s. Common.* Value: per card, $2.

p/Sborgi	$3–$10
Sherlock Holmes	$2–$20
Star Trek (l.c.)	$1–$5

STATE GIRLS (e.c.)	*$8–$20*
p/Langsdorf	*$10–$12*
p/Langsdorf, silk appliqué dress	
	$25–$35
p/National Art	*$8–$10*
p/Platinachrome	*$10–$12*
p/Tuck, ser 2669	*$8–$10*
p/Stengle	*$3–$10*
SUNBONNET BABIES (e.c.)	*$5–$20*

"Thursday" from the series of seven Sunbonnet designs by H. I. Robbins of Boston. This series is less common than those drawn by Wall. Value: $20.

SUPERHEROES (l.c.)	*$1–$5*
UNICORNS (l.c.)	*$1–$3*
Vegetable Heads p/Zieher (e.c.)	*$6*
WITCHES (e.c.)	*$6–$60*
WIZARD OF OZ (l.c.)	*$1–$2*
Yellow Kid (e.c.), s/R. F. Outcault	*$50–$75*

HISTORY AND POLITICS

The History and Politics section focuses primarily on postcards of American political and social history and secondly on European political history. Postcards of famous leaders, presidents, presidential elections, royal families, wars, patriotism, and political struggles, structures, and boundaries are all found in this section.

Campaign postcards, especially third-party presidential candidates, are eagerly sought. Third-party campaign postcards are always valued higher than Democratic or Republican candidates.

The most abundant campaign postcards are from the 1908 contest between William Taft and William Jennings Bryan. Chrome-finish postcards of Richard Nixon and his family are particularly common among more recent postcards.

Some early presidential series are particularly fine quality but lack collector appeal because coverage reaches only to Woodrow Wilson. Modern postcards (both satiric and serious) of recent presidents are popular: Carter, Reagan, and Bush.

Social movements (labor, black equality, women's suffrage) and their backlash (anti-semitism, Ku Klux Klan, violence against women) are seriously collected for the purpose of documentation of social change. This topic has high potential for continued increases in value.

In the listings which follow, all figures represent values for individual postcards (not for an entire series).

HISTORY AND POLITICS VALUES

Aesop's Fables, s/F. Sancha, p/Tuck (satire)	
	$20–$25
America's famous men, p/Austen	$12–$15
ANTI-SEMITISM	$5–$75

Courtesy of Jonah Shapiro

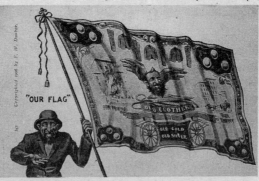

An excellent example of anti-Semitism. Undivided back, copyright 1906 by F. W. Dunbar. Rare. Value: $60.

BICENTENNIAL (1976)	$2–$10
BILLY POSSUM	$2–$20
s/Crite	$10–$20
s/Dewees	$15–$18
p/Lounsbury, ser 2515, 2517	$15–$20
BLACK LEADERS	$2–$20
BOER WAR (e.c.)	$10–$50
Empire series, p/Tuck	$18–$25
Bonus Army Expeditionary Force (m.c.)	
	$10–$20
British Royal Family (pio)	$15–$30
British Royal Family (e.c.)	$8–$20
British Royal Family (m.c.)	$2–$20
British Royal Family (l.c.)	$1–$4
BUSH, GEORGE (l.c.)	$1–$3
CARTER, JIMMY (l.c.)	$1–$3
CAVELL, EDITH (e.c.)	$5–$40
Colonial heroes, p/Schwalback	$10–$12
DEBBS, EUGENE (Amer. Socialist Pres. cand.)	
	$200–$1,000
Donaldson American heroes	$12–$15
EQUAL RIGHTS AMENDMENT (l.c.)	$2–$10

From the author's collection

The campaign to pass the Equal Rights Amendment attracted wide participation by the American public. The quilts, postcards, and other articles document the involvement of many people. Completed by the League of Women Voters of Oakland, California, 1981. Not common. Value: $4.

FAB PATCHWORK (royalty)	$20–$30
FLAGS (e.c.)	$5–$15
FORD, GERALD (l.c.)	$1–$3
GREAT WHITE FLEET	$10–$150

Uncle Sam's Warships, accordion fold

$150

Heroes of the South, ser 2510, p/Tuck

$10–$12

HITLER, ADOLF (m.c.)	$5–$20

Courtesy of Postcard Collector

Adolf Hitler; one of a series of drawings of Nazi leaders repro-duced on postcards. Artist-signed KB. Not common. Value: $12.

The minimum value in this price guide is $1. While many dealers offer 25-cent and 50-cent "bargain boxes," few dealers sort, individually price, and protectively "sleeve" postcards valued at less than $1. This price guide offers values for postcards worth $1 or more.

INDIAN LEADERS (e.c.) $2–$20
    p/Illustrated Postcard, ser 77 $6–$10
    Indian Chiefs, ser 2171, p/Tuck $12–$15

Courtesy of Fred Schiffman

Chief White Swan. A Tuck "Oilette" postcard, "Indian Chiefs"
#3495. Not common. Value: $18.

JOHNSON, LYNDON B. (m.c.) $2–$10
KENNEDY, JOHN F. (m.c.) $2–$10

From the author's collection

Standard-size chrome view of the assassination site of President
Kennedy with two inset details. Produced by the Texas Postcard &
Novelty Co., 1960s. Common. Value: $4.

KING, MARTIN LUTHER (m.c.) $2–$20
Kings and Queens of England, p/Tuck
$12–$15

Courtesy of John and Sandy Millns

"Edward V," from Raphael Tuck & Sons "Kings and Queens of England" series 615. As with many undivided-back postcards published by Tuck, this was designed in England but "chromographed in Germany." The complete set consists of twelve cards each in series 614, 615, and 616, plus a single card in series 617. Scarce. Value: $15.

KU KLUX KLAN $20–$200

Courtesy of John and Sandy Millns

Real photo postcard of four hooded Ku Klux Klan members in a flag-decked automobile. The plate on the front is dated 1928. The markings on the headlights read, "One School. One Flag." Rare. Value: $150.

LINCOLN, ABRAHAM (e.c.) $2–$25
    p/Anglo American: Open Book ser 726
                             $20–$25
    p/Anglo American: Open Book ser 727
                             $18–$20
    p/Nash, ser 2, woman and torn flag
                             $10–$12
    p/Nash, "Lincoln Centennial Souvenir"
                             $8–$10
    p/Taggart, ser 606 $8–$10
    p/Tuck, ser 155 $10–$12
MCKINLEY, mourning (e.c.) $10–$15
MEXICAN BORDER DISPUTE (e.c.) $5–$20

Real photo view of riflemen posed by railroad siding, one of many incidents from the Mexican border dispute recorded on film and reproduced on postcards. Copyright 1914 by E. E. Denn. Not common. Value: $7.

    p/Horne $10–$20
    p/International Film Service $5–$10
    p/Kavanaugh War Postals $5–$10
MUSSOLINI, BENITO (m.c.) $5–$20
NIXON, RICHARD (m.c.) $2–$10
Papal Illuminated Popes, p/Ferloni $6–$10
PRESIDENTIAL CAMPAIGN 1900 $35–$300
PRESIDENTIAL CAMPAIGN 1904 $30–$100

PRESIDENTIAL CAMPAIGN 1908 $10–$300

From the author's collection

"The National Choice" shows 1908 Republican candidates Taft and Sherman. An identical design shows Democratic candidates Bryan and Kern. A common set for the 1908 campaign, published by H. M. Rose Co. Value: $15.

Bryan-Kern	$10–$75
Taft/Bryan	$10–$200
Taft/Sherman	$10–$50
Third party candidates	$20–$300
PRESIDENTIAL CAMPAIGN 1912	$12–$125
PRESIDENTIAL CAMPAIGN 1916	$20–$100
PRESIDENTIAL CAMPAIGN 1920	$15–$250
PRESIDENTIAL CAMPAIGN 1924	$40–$125
PRESIDENTIAL CAMPAIGN 1928	$40–$75
PRESIDENTIAL CAMPAIGN 1932	$15–$70
PRESIDENTIAL CAMPAIGN 1936, 1940, 1944	
	$15–$85
PRESIDENTIAL CAMPAIGN 1948	$15–$75
PRESIDENTIAL CAMPAIGN 1952, 1956	$5–$35
PRESIDENTIAL CAMPAIGN 1960	$8–$30
PRESIDENTIAL CAMPAIGN 1964	$3–$25
PRESIDENTIAL CAMPAIGN 1968, 1972	$2–$8
PRESIDENTIAL CAMPAIGN 1976	$2–$10
PRESIDENTIAL CAMPAIGN 1980, 1984, 1988	
	$1–$10
PRESIDENTS' HOMES, p/Tuck	$10–$12
PROHIBITION/TEMPERANCE	$8–$20
REAGAN, RONALD (l.c.)	$1–$10

ROOSEVELT, FRANKLIN D. (m.c.)   *$6–$40*

Courtesy of John and Sandy Millns

*... a dir le mie virtu
basta un sorriso...*

*Italian propaganda postcard with anti-American sentiments.
Very rare. Value: $40 or more.*

ROOSEVELT, THEODORE (e.c.)   *$8–$50*

Courtesy of John and Sandy Millns

*Theodore Roosevelt in Panama, November 1906. Part of the cap-
tion reads, "Note that the President is without glasses." Undivided
back. Not common. Value: $25.*

Alice Roosevelt	$10–$20
Cartoons, esp with Teddy bears	$10–$50
Family portraits	$8–$10
Portraits	$8–$20
Roosevelt-Longworth wedding	$10–$15
Roosevelt's African hunt, c/Underwood	$8–$10
Roosevelt in Africa, p/Cromwell	$8–$10
Roosevelt Tour, c/Arthur Capper	$10–$12

ROYALTY (pio.)	$15–$50
ROYALTY (e.c.)	$10–$50

From the author's collection

Ludwig II, King of Bavaria, 1845–1886. Novelty postcard: molded celluloid frame of flowers, covered with acetate, real edelweiss and foliage enclosed. Scarce. Value: $30.

ROYALTY (m.c.)	$2–$30
ROYALTY (l.c.)	$1–$10
Rulers of the World, p/Alt	$8–$12
RUSSO-JAPANESE WAR, Portsmouth Treaty	
	$8–$20
Sheridan's Ride	$5–$6

Remember! All prices in this guide represent postcards in *Excellent* condition.

SPANISH AMERICAN WAR (pio.) $2–$20
     p/Browning (pio.), Camp Harvey $35–$50
     p/Kropp, Camp Harvey, Camp Thomas
                                  $35–$50
     p/Rost $25–$35
     p/Stratton $15– $20
     p/Universal Postal Card (pio.) $35–$40

Courtesy of Fred Schiffman

A postcard on the Spanish American War produced by a German firm, Max Marcus of Berlin, for the German market. Mailed April 2, 1898, and received April 28, 1898. Rare. Value: $50.

TAFT, WILLIAM HOWARD (e.c.) $8–$30
     Cartoons $12–$20
     Commemoratives $20–$30
     Inaugural $8–$10
     Portraits $8–$12
     Presidential visit to Italy, real photo
                                  $8–$10
     Real photos $8–$10

The minimum value in this price guide is $1. While many dealers offer 25-cent and 50-cent "bargain boxes," few dealers sort, individually price, and protectively "sleeve" postcards valued at less than $1. This price guide offers values for postcards worth $1 or more.

U.S. Army, ser 404, p/Tuck	$10–$12
U.S. Navy, ser 405, p/Tuck	$10–$12
U.S. PRESIDENTS (e.c.)	$6–$10
s/Paul Dubosclard, p/Sheehan (m.c.)	
	$6–$8
Flag & Eagle Presidents	$5–$6
s/Morris Katz (l.c.)	$3
p/Leighton	$5–$6
"Makers of America" series	$4–$6
p/Numismatic Card (l.c.)	$1
p/Philadelphia PC	$5–$6
p/Tuck	$6–$10

Courtesy of John and Sandy Millns

President Andrew Johnson. Published by Raphael Tuck & Sons, "Presidents of the United States," series 2328. Johnson postcards are among the least common of presidential postcards. Artist-signed L. P. Spinner. Value: $10.

VIETNAM WAR	$2–$10

WASHINGTON, GEORGE   *$2–$20*
    p/Anglo American, Open Book ser 725
       $15–$20
    p/Anglo American, Open Book ser 728
       $12–$18
    p/International Art   *$5–$12*
    p/Nash   *$5–$12*
    p/Tuck   *$5–$10*

From the author's collection

George Washington, first President of the United States. From the Tuck series 2328, "Presidents of the United States." Common. Value: $8.

p/Whitney   *$5–$8*

WILD BILL HICKOK (e.c.) $8–$10

From the author's collection

A multi-image design honors frontiersman Wild Bill Hickok. Combination portrait, Art Nouveau decoration, view, and descriptive material in one design. Divided back, copyright and published by W. B. Perkins, Jr., Lead, South Dakota. Not common. Value: $10.

WOMEN'S SUFFRAGE	$10–$50
p/Cargill, #1–110, #112–122	$20–$25
p/Cargill, #123–130	$25–$35
p/Cargill, #111	$200

From the author's collection

Card #111, the rare one, from the Cargill series of thirty postcards. The first twenty show identical designs, each with a different statement. Cards 21–30 show flags and other patriotic imagery with more suffrage statements. Rare. Value: $200.

p/Dunston-Weiler	$20–$35
s/Walter Wellman	$30–$35

"*Our next Presidentess,*" card #4,000 of the sixteen-card series signed by Walter Wellman. Scarce. Value: $35.

WORLD WAR I	$2–$20
p/Bamforth, comics	$5–$20
p/*Chicago Daily News* (Kavanaugh War Postals)	$4–$6
p/Daily Mail	$4–$8
p/Noyer	$10–$20
p/Photochrom	$5–$15
p/Salvation Army	$3–$6
s/Xavier Sager	$20–$30
p/Tuck	$5–$20

Remember! All prices in this guide represent postcards in *Excellent* condition.

WORLD WAR II	$1–$25
p/Asheville Post Card	$2–$5
s/Dave Breger	$5–$10
p/Hoffmann	$10–$20
p/Kropp	$1–$10
p/MWM	$1–$10
s/Donald McGill	$5–$15
Nazi-German propaganda	$5–$30
s/Harry Payne	$10–$20
s/Louis Raemakers	$10–$25
p/Teich	$1–$10
p/Thompson	$5–$10

From the author's collection

Linen-style color postcard of a USO club operated by the Salvation Army. Published by the Supplies and Purchasing Department of the Salvation Army, Atlanta, Georgia; printed by Curt Teich. Not common. Value: $4.

MISCELLANEOUS

The Miscellaneous section includes postcards on religious subjects, unique sets and series such as stamps and coins, and a variety of novelty and other oddball postcards.

There are many Lord's Prayer and Ten Commandments postcards but few are popular today. The pioneer-period Passion Play postcards are valued for their age.

Stamp and coin postcards track the popularity of those hobbies, both of which are currently regaining strength.

Novelty postcards are collected because they are so unusual or because of their tie-ins to various subjects such as Santas,

Halloween, or Teddy bears. Their odd shapes and sizes make them difficult to store; this has affected their desirability for many collectors. Many novelty postcards are underpriced relative to their supply and subject matter.

In the listings which follow, all values are for early-century (e.c., 1898–1918) postcards unless stated otherwise.

MISCELLANEOUS VALUES

AIRBRUSH	$2–$12
ALPHABETS	$2–$20

Courtesy of John and Sandy Millns

The letter "N" from the Floral Alphabet Series, artist-signed C. Klein. Pre–World War I. Scarce. Value: $20.

ATTACHMENTS	$2–$30

From the author's collection

A spring-wire tail attachment. Several animals appear on postcards with spring-wire tail attachments. The politically oriented designs are more valuable. Not common. Value: $8.

From the author's collection

The features and clothing on this photo postcard of a beautiful woman have been brightly tinted. Rick-rack and sequins have been attached over her hair to make a hat, a symbol frequently associated with St. Catherine's Day. A "Ste. Catherine" greeting has been gold-foil stamped near the bottom of the card. Scarce. Value: $35.

BLOCK PRINTS	$2–$20
BOOK MARKS, p/Tuck	$8–$10
BUTTON ATTACHMENTS	$12–$20
CELLULOID	$2–$30
COIN (gold-foil stamped)	$10–$25
COIN ATTACHMENTS	$2–$5
COINS (as subject)	$2–$20
COPPER (postcards made of copper)	$1–$5
CORALENE (tiny beads)	$2–$10

The minimum value in this price guide is $1. While many dealers offer 25-cent and 50-cent "bargain boxes," few dealers sort, individually price, and protectively "sleeve" postcards valued at less than $1. This price guide offers values for postcards worth $1 or more.

CUT-OUTS $50–$200

Courtesy of Postcard Collector

A paper doll cut-out. "Marion," one of several produced as advertising postcards for F. Mayer Boot & Shoe Co. of Milwaukee. Pre–World War I. Very rare. Value: $100.

DIE-CUT HOLD-TO-LIGHT (e.c)	$15–$1,000
Christmas	$20–$40
Easter	$15–$25
p/Kohler	$20–$75
New Years	$15–$30
St. Louis Exposition	$30–$100
St. Louis Exposition, Inside Inn	$100
Santas	$150–$250
Uncle Sam Santas	$1,000
Valentines	$15–$25
Year-Dates	$15–$25
DIE-CUT HOLD-TO-LIGHTS (l.c.), p/Avis	$5–$8
EMBOSSED	$3–$20

Remember! All prices in this guide represent postcards in *Excellent* condition.

EMBROIDERY—GREETINGS	*$8–$20*
EMBROIDERY—PATRIOTIC	*$15–$50*
EMBROIDERY—SHIPS	*$40–$100*

Courtesy of Fred Schiffman

Embroidered flag and foliage with a photo inset of President Wilson, produced in France for World War I American troops. The fabric is framed with embossed white stock. Scarce. Value: $50.

ESPERANTO	*$3–$30*
FELT ATTACHMENTS	*$2–$8*
FLOWER ATTACHMENTS	*$5–$20*
FORTUNE/HOROSCOPE (e.c.)	*$8–$15*
FORTUNE/HOROSCOPE (m.c.)	*$1–$6*
FORTUNE/HOROSCOPE (l.c.)	*$1–$3*
FUR ATTACHMENTS	*$5–$15*
GLASS EYE ATTACHMENTS	*$2–$12*
HAIR ATTACHMENTS—WOMEN	*$15–$25*
HAIR ATTACHMENTS—SANTAS	*$50–$150*
HAND-MADE	*$1–$20*
HONEYCOMB	*$10–$20*
HYGROSCOPE (weather forecaster)	*$2–$10*

INSTALLMENTS/COMPOSITES (price per card)

	$10–$50
Hearst cartoons (per set)	$80–$100
p/Huld, Santa, Uncle Sam	$50–$60
p/Huld, other	$20–$25
Napoleon, Joan of Arc (per set)	$350–$500
LARGE LETTER (e.c.)	$2–$20
LARGE LETTER (m.c.)	$1–$5
LEATHER	$2–$20
LORD'S PRAYER	$8–$15

From the author's collection

Child and angel designs from series of eight Lord's Prayer post-cards. Embossed foil highlights the designs. Pre–WWI. Not common. Value: $10.

MACERATED MONEY (e.c.) $100–$200

Courtesy of John and Sandy Millns

Macerated money postcard. Card stock without flecks. Pre–World War I. Postal usage and card stock type affect value. Value: used, $150–$300; unused, $100–$200.

MACERATED MONEY (l.c.)	$5
MAPS (e.c.)	$2–$20
MAPS (m.c.)	$1–$10
MAPS (l.c.)	$1–$3
MATCHBOOK	$5–$15

From the author's collection

Matchbook postcard. World War II period. Many of the designs have military base or troop tie-ins. Not common. Value: $15.

MAXIMUM	$2–$20

The minimum value in this price guide is $1. While many dealers offer 25-cent and 50-cent "bargain boxes," few dealers sort, individually price, and protectively "sleeve" postcards valued at less than $1. This price guide offers values for postcards worth $1 or more.

MECHANICAL (e.c.)	$10–$200
Advertising	$50–$200
s/Clapsaddle	$15–$200
Pinwheels	$20–$200

From the author's collection

Rare linen mechanical produced by Curt Teich of Chicago for McCormick Photographers of Amarillo, Texas. The card promotes the Grande Court of Amarillo. The "mechanical" feature is the cut-out woman loosely riveted to the card so that she rocks back and forth on the horse. Rare. Value: $50.

METAL ATTACHMENTS	$2–$15
MOTHER-OF-PEARL	$2–$10
MULTIPLE-PANEL FOLDS (e.c.)	$2–$50
Advertising	$5–$50
Views	$2–$30

Remember! All prices in this guide represent postcards in *Excellent* condition.

Courtesy of Fred Schiffman

Multiple-use postcard. This example has room for four addresses and four messages. It was mailed four times in 1908. Scarce. Value: $30.

OBERAMMERGAU (pio.)	$10–$20
PAINTING BOOKS (Tuck postcard painting albums)	
	$35–$50
PAPER DOLLS	$50–$250
PASSION PLAY (e.c.)	$2–$15
PASSION PLAY (m.c.)	$1–$3
PASSION PLAY (l.c.)	$1–$2
PERFORATED—GLAMOUR/TOPICS	$5–$25

Perforations have been run through the card stock at horizontal and vertical angles. It was meant to be torn apart and re-assembled as a puzzle. Pre–World War I, scarce. Value: $20.

PERFORATED—VIEWS	$2–$15
PHONOGRAPH RECORDS, p/Tuck, Gramophone	
	$5–$15
PIN CUSHION	$2–$10
PUNCH-OUTS, p/Tuck	$15–$18
REBUS	$2–$15
REWARD (for "Wanted" criminals)	$2–$12
RIBBON ATTACHMENTS	$2–$8
SILHOUETTE	$3–$20

SILK APPLIQUÉ—SANTAS $30–$50

Santa's suit and the reindeer cinch have silk cloth attached over the printed design. Pre–World War I. Scarce. Value: $50.

SILK APPLIQUÉ—COLLEGE GIRLS $30–$35
SILK APPLIQUÉ—STATE GIRLS $30–$35

An example from the popular State Girls Series. The skirt is overlaid with silk. Pre–World War I. Scarce. Value: $30.

SILK PRINTING ON FABRIC $5–$100
SONGS $2–$15
SPRING-WIRE ATTACHMENTS $5–$30

| SQUEAKERS (e.c.) | $20–$150 |
| SQUEAKERS (m.c.) | $5–$20 |

From the author's collection

A chrome-finish 1960s' "squeaker" alligator that makes noise when squeezed. This example also has a moving "glass-eye" attachment. Common. Value: $6.

STAMPS (e.c.)	$2–$12
p/Zieher embossed	$20–$40
p/Zieher, embossed, U.S.	$25
p/Zieher, not embossed	$10–$15

Courtesy of *Postcard Collector*

U.S. postage stamps on an Ottmar Zieher issue. The flat postcards were printed later than the embossed and are valued lower. Reproducing facsimile U.S. stamps on postcards was prohibited so this example is not common. Value: $15.

TEN COMMANDMENTS	$8–$20
TIED CHRISTMAS SEALS	$3–$50
TRANSPARENCY HOLD-TO-LIGHT	$15–$80
WOOD	$2–$15
WOVEN SILK	$20–$150

NATURE, AND BASIC AND APPLIED SCIENCE

This section includes images of science and nature, both photographed and realistic artist-drawn images. It also includes postcards on scientific investigation and practical applications of science.

Postcards of animals have always been very popular. Large numbers have survived, especially of animals in zoos; prices are consequently low. A combination of rarity and greater demand supports higher prices of top-quality artist-drawn images of nature.

In modern postcards, space exploration is particularly popular. Industry and manufacturing postcards of all periods are not common, though this relative scarcity is not fully reflected in their price.

NATURE, AND BASIC AND APPLIED SCIENCE VALUES

AGRICULTURE   *$1–$20*

Courtesy of Joel Edler

Real photo view, unloading potatoes, Iola, Wisconsin. Postally used, 1907. Scarce. Value: $20.

AMPHIBIANS	*$1–$10*
ANTARCTICA	*$2–$20*
ARCHITECTURE	*$5–$20*
ASTRONOMY/TELESCOPES	*$2–$10*
BIRDS	*$1–$15*
DuPont Powders (e.c., birds)	$50–$60
p/Tuck, ser 402 (e.c.)	$10–$12

BUFFALO	$1–$10
BUTTERFLIES	$1–$10
p/Tuck, ser 403 (e.c.)	$8–$10
CATS (e.c.), realistic images	$3–$20
Real photo	$3–$20
CATS (m.c.)	$1–$5
CATS (l.c.)	$1–$3
DIONNE QUINTUPLETS	$1–$20

Courtesy of *Postcard Collector*

The Dionne quintuplets of Callender, Ontario. Not common. Value: $15.

DOGS	$3–$20
p/DuPont Powders (dogs, e.c.)	$60–$75

Courtesy of Joel Edler

Manitoba Rap, a 1909 champion. The series of artist-drawn Edm. H. Osthaus dogs advertising DuPont Powders is desired by collectors for their advertising, dogs, and artist-drawn aspects. Scarce. Value: $65.

DOGS (m.c.)	$2–$10
DOGS (l.c.)	$1–$3

DOMESTIC ANIMALS, p/Tuck	$10–$12
EARTHQUAKES	$2–$10
ELEPHANTS	$1–$10
FARM ANIMALS	$1–$10
FISH	$3–$10
FLOODS	$2–$15
FROGS	$3–$10
HALLEY'S COMET	$5–$40

Courtesy of *Postcard Collector*

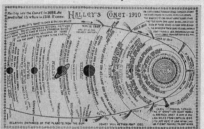

Halley's Comet, 1910. A celestial map showing the path of Halley's Comet. Copyright 1910 by J. W. Donaldson, St. Paul. Scarce. Value: $35.

HORSES (e.c.) realistic images	$3–$20
s/Hary Payne	$6–$40
Real photo	$1–$25
HORSES (m.c.)	$1–$15
HORSES (l.c.)	$1–$3
LABORATORIES	$2–$40
MANUFACTURING	$2–$40
MEDICINE	$2–$10

From the author's collection

Modern drug manufacture. Chrome-finish postcard, 1960s. Value: $4.

MINING (e.c.)	$2–$10
Real photo	$5–$25

Pre–World War I real photo of the fifth level, Independence Mine. Photo by Skolds. Scarce. Value: $15.

MT. ST. HELEN'S (l.c.)	$1–$2
NORTH POLE	$10–$40

North Pole exploration by Frederick Cook and Robert Peary. Scarce. Value: $25.

NUCLEAR POWER	$1–$5
PANDAS (m.c.)	$2–$15
PANDAS (l.c.)	$1–$3

PLANTLIFE (e.c.)	$1–$15
PLANTLIFE (m.c.)	$1–$3
PLANTLIFE (l.c.)	$1
REPTILES	$1–$10
SPACE EXPLORATION (m.c.)	$2–$10
SPACE EXPLORATION (l.c.)	$1–$5

From the author's collection

Standard-size chrome-finish view of five astronauts in space.
Common. Value: $2.

TORNADOS	$2–$30
VOLCANOS	$1–$10
WILD ANIMALS, p/Tuck, ser 401	$10–$12

Courtesy of John and Sandy Millns

Artist-drawn zebra, #2 from the Wild Animal Series published by
Raphael Tuck & Sons. Not common. Value: $10.

ZOOS (e.c.)	$1–$5
ZOOS (m.c.)	$1–$2
ZOOS (l.c.)	$1–$2

POSTCARD-RELATED

Postcards about postcards is a special topic unique to the hobby. This section covers postcards on the creation, manufacture, distribution, and use of postcards. Also included are postcards about and by postcard collectors.

Early hobby-related postcards are scarce and avidly sought, and values reflect this demand. Unusual postcard Americana is especially desirable.

From the late 1940s to the present, collectors and clubs have produced many postcards about their shows, clubs, and collecting activities; to mark current events and commemorate historic events; and in celebration of National Postcard Week. As with other contemporary postcards, only the best designs are likely to retain their value as collectibles.

POSTCARD-RELATED VALUES

p/All States Hobby Club (1960s)	$1–$3
AMERICANA	$2–$50

Courtesy of John and Sandy Millns

Remarkable example of postcard Americana—a woman on roller skates wearing a postcard hat and dress! Real photo postcard from Kolb Bros. Studio, pre–World War I. Value: $75 or more!

s/Rick Geary	*$1–$5*
s/E. Gorey	*$3–$5*
p/Bob Hendricks	*$5–$10*

From the author's collection

Card #P9-49, published in 1949 by Bob Hendricks for the Post Card Collectors Club, is a commemorative reproduction of a postcard from 1908. Not common. Value: $6.

Hermann, Emanuel (commemorative)   *$150*

Courtesy of John and Sandy Millns

Emanuel Hermann originated the idea for postcards. This example of the 1894 commemorative celebrating the 25-year anniversary of postcards is autographed and numbered. Value: $150.

s/Shirley Kemp	*$1–$2*
p/Metropolitan Post Card Club (1947–present)	
	$1–$5
NATIONAL POSTCARD WEEK (1984–present)	*$1–$5*
POSTCARD CLUBS CARDS (1940s–present)	*$1–$5*

POSTCARD DISTRIBUTORS/MANUFACTURERS (e.c.)
$30–$150

POSTCARD DISTRIBUTORS/MANUFACTURERS (m.c.)
$1–$30

POSTCARD DISTRIBUTORS/MANUFACTURERS (l.c.)
$1–$10

POSTCARD EXPOSITIONS/SHOWS (e.c.) $100–$200

POSTCARD EXPOSITIONS/SHOWS (m.c.) $1–$5

POSTCARD EXPOSITIONS/SHOWS (l.c.) $1–$3

Courtesy of John and Sandy Millns

Real photo view of a postcard wagon for Thrifty Foto Service, a processing service for photographic postcards. Very rare. Value: $150.

From the author's collection

Linen-finish view of the manufacturing plant for Curt Teich & Co., the largest publisher of mid-century postcards in the United States. Not common. Value: $15.

Remember! All prices in this guide represent postcards in *Excellent* condition.

Chrome-finish view of Dexter Mfg. plant, a major American publisher of chrome-finish views. Not common. When postcard publishers' price lists are printed on the back, the value may be increased slightly. Value: $15.

POSTCARD MERCHANDISING (e.c., real photo)

$10–$75

Real photo view of a dry goods store interior features a ferris wheel display unit for the postcards. Rare. Value: $75.

p/Presiosi Postcards	$1–$10
s/Ann Rusnak	$1–$2
p/Western Reserve Postcard Society	$1–$3
p/Wichita Post Card Club	$1–$5
p/Windy City Postcard Club	$1–$2

TRANSPORTATION

Transportation postcards on all subjects of all ages are popular with collectors. Vast quantities of modern postcards are produced; prices are the same as for other modern postcards. Older postcards, especially real photo views of depots and railroads, aircraft, and motor and water transport are avidly sought and prices continue to rise.

Early-century (e.c.), mid-century (m.c.), and late-century (l.c.) modifiers refer to the age of the postcards, not of the subjects pictured.

AIR TRANSPORTATION VALUES

AIR MEETS (e.c.)	$10–$35
AIR MEETS (m.c.)	$2–$12
AIRPORTS (e.c.)	$2–$10
AIRPORTS (m.c.)	$2–$5
AIRPORTS (l.c.)	$1–$3
BI-PLANES	$2–$20
BLIMPS (m.c.)	$5–$20
BLIMPS (l.c.)	$1–$3
CONCORD	$1–$2
EARHART, AMELIA	$5–$35
HELICOPTERS (m.c.)	$5–$20
HELICOPTERS (l.c.)	$1–$5
HINDENBERG (m.c.)	$10–$150
HOT-AIR BALLOONS	$1–$15

The minimum value in this price guide is $1. While many dealers offer 25-cent and 50-cent "bargain boxes," few dealers sort, individually price, and protectively "sleeve" postcards valued at less than $1. This price guide offers values for postcards worth $1 or more.

INTERIORS (m.c.) $5–$15

Interior of a Pan Am 747, late 1960s, on a chrome-finish advertising postcard. Not common. Value: $5.

INTERIORS (l.c.)	$1–$5
JET AIRCRAFT, FOREIGN AIRLINES	$1–$4
ADVERTISING POSTCARDS	$2–$10
JET AIRCRAFT, U.S. AIRLINES	$1–$4
ADVERTISING POSTCARDS	$2–$10
LINDBERGH, CHARLES	$2–$35

Real photo postcard, and Oxley photo of Lindbergh at Fargo, North Dakota. Rare. Value: $25.

MENUS (m.c.)	$2–$15
MILITARY AIRCRAFT (m.c.)	$2–$15
MILITARY AIRCRAFT (l.c.)	$1–$4
MUSEUM POSTCARDS (m.c.)	$1–$8
MUSEUM POSTCARDS (l.c.)	$1–$3

PROPELLER AIRCRAFT, FOREIGN AIRLINES	$1–$5
ADVERTISING POSTCARDS	$2–$25
PROPELLER AIRCRAFT, U.S. AIRLINES	$1–$4
ADVERTISING POSTCARDS	$2–$20

Courtesy of Joel Edler

Above: A BRANIFF AIR-WAYS Lockheed "Elec-tra" in flight—wheels up. Two pilots, two engines.

Left: Luxurious cabin of a BRANIFF AIRWAYS "Electra" equipped with individual ventilators, reading lamps and ash trays.

Black and white undersize (3⅛ × 5⅜ inches) advertising postcard, and interior and exterior multiview of Braniff Airways' Lockheed Electra, a twin-engine plane. Probably late 1940s, as the stamp box indicates that only one cent postage was required. Not common. Value: $12.

SKYDIVING (l.c.)	$1–$5
p/Tuck, ser 406, Educational Series	$15–$20
p/Tuck, other	$8–$15
ZEPPELINS	$20–$150

Remember! All prices in this guide represent postcards in *Excellent* condition.

RAIL TRANSPORTATION VALUES

ADVERTISING (e.c.)	$3–$15
ADVERTISING (m.c.)	$1–$10

Courtesy of Joel Edler

*Advertising postcard for the Burlington Route's Denver Zephyr—
diesel-powered, made of stainless steel. Printed in two colors.
Postally used 1949. Not common. Value: $8.*

ADVERTISING (l.c.)	$1–$5
Chicago & Alton (St. Louis World's Fair)	
	$20–$30
DEPOTS (e.c.)	$3–$20
Real photo	$15–$80
DEPOTS (m.c.)	$1–$5
DEPOTS (l.c.)	$1–$3
INTERIORS (e.c.)	$5–$15
INTERIORS (m.c.)	$2–$12

Courtesy of Joel Edler

*Two interior views of the tavern/lunch counter in a Chicago/North
Western line Streamliner 400. A linen-finish postcard, published
by Curt Teich in 1939. Not common. Value: $12.*

Interior view of the lounge on a chrome-finish ad postcard from Union Pacific RR. 1950s. Not common. Value: $6.

INTERIORS (l.c.)	*$1–$5*
RAILROADS, FOREIGN (e.c.)	*$5–$25*
Real photo	*$5–$35*
RAILROADS, FOREIGN (m.c.)	*$1–$10*
RAILROADS, FOREIGN (l.c.)	*$1–$2*
RAILROADS, U.S. (e.c.)	*$5–$40*
Real photo	*$10–$50*
RAILROADS, U.S. (m.c.)	*$1–$10*
RAILROADS, U.S. (l.c.)	*$1–$5*

A current-issue continental-size view of steam-driven locomotives at Cass Scenic Railroad State Park in West Virginia. Copyright Ron and Linda Card, Cards Unlimited. Value: 30¢–50¢

ROCK ISLAND LINE (adv, s/O'Neill)	*$50–$75*
SCENIC RAILROADS (e.c.)	*$1–$2*
SUBWAYS	*$1–$10*
TRAIN WRECKS	*$2–$20*

TROLLEYS (e.c.)	$10–$30
Real photo	$15–$75
TROLLEYS (m.c.)	$2–$20
TROLLEYS (l.c.)	$1–$3

Courtesy of *Postcard Collector*

Electric trolley on a dirt street in Newtown, Pennsylvania. Real photo postcard. Scarce. Value: $30.

TROLLEYS, HORSE-DRAWN	$2–$40

ROAD TRANSPORTATION VALUES

ACCIDENTS (real photo)	$3–$15
ADVERTISING (other products using autos)	
	$10–$100

Courtesy of Joel Edler

The novelty of early automobiles made them an eye-catching subject for advertising other products, as on this postcard promoting the Conrad Seipp Brewing Co. of Chicago. A rare and highly desirable postcard. Value: $80.

AUTO ADVERTISING (e.c.)	*$10–$50*
AUTO ADVERTISING (1930s)	*$5–$30*
AUTO ADVERTISING (1940s)	*$4–$25*

Courtesy of Joel Edler

Advertising for a 1947 Pontiac. Not common. Value: $8.

AUTO ADVERTISING (1950s)	*$2–$15*

Courtesy of Joel Edler

The Edsel advertising postcard has a product endorsement by Kim Novak. Not common. Value: $8.

AUTO ADVERTISING (1960s)	*$2–$10*
AUTO ADVERTISING (1970–80s)	*$1–$5*
AUTO RACING (e.c.)	*$10–$100*
AUTO RACING (m.c.)	*$2–$20*
AUTO RACING (l.c.)	*$1–$10*
BUSES/BUS DEPOTS (e.c.)	*$3–$30*
Real photo	*$5–$40*
BUSES/BUS DEPOTS (m.c.)	*$2–$20*
BUSES/BUS DEPOTS (l.c.)	*$1–$5*

DEALERSHIPS (e.c.)	$5–$40
DEALERSHIPS (m.c.)	$5–$25

Courtesy of Joel Edler

A garage/gas station/dealership, the Dodgeville Motor Co. of Wisconsin, is shown on this 1930s(?) real photo postcard. Trucks are seldom seen on postcards. Rare. Value: $25.

DEALERSHIPS (l.c.)	$1–$5
DELIVERY VEHICLES, HORSE-DRAWN	$5–$20
Real photo	$10–$100
DELIVERY VEHICLES, MOTORIZED (e.c.)	$5–$35
DELIVERY VEHICLES, MOTORIZED (m.c.)	$2–$10

Courtesy of *Postcard Collector*

This advertising for Johns Service funeral parlors shows a fine example of a mid-century delivery vehicle—a hearse. Published by Curt Teich in 1942. Rare. Value: $20.

DELIVERY VEHICLES, MOTORIZED (l.c.)	$1–$5

FACTORIES $5–$40

Courtesy of Joel Edler

Multi-image advertising postcard for Indian Motorcycles shows the Springfield, Massachusetts, factory, a motorcycle, and the company logo. Linen-finish, probably 1930s. A rare and desirable postcard. Value: $35.

GARAGES/GAS STATIONS (e.c.)	$2–$10
Real photo	$8–$50
GARAGES/GAS STATIONS (m.c.)	$2–$10
GARAGES/GAS STATIONS (m.c.)	$1–$3
HORSE-DRAWN (e.c., noncommercial)	$1–$5
Real photo	$3–$10
LINCOLN HIGHWAY (m.c.)	$2–$8
MOTORCYCLES (e.c.)	$5–$20
Real photo	$15–$50

Courtesy of Fred Schiffman

Real photo view by Oxley of Indian Motorcycles. Rare. Value: $30.

MOTORCYCLES (m.c.)	$3–$35
MOTORCYCLES (l.c.)	$2–$8

PENNSYLVANIA TURNPIKE (m.c.)	*$1–$3*
REAL PHOTOS (e.c.)	*$5–$50*
REAL PHOTOS (m.c.)	*$2–$20*
REAL PHOTOS (l.c.)	*$1–$10*
ROUTE 66 (m.c.)	*$1–$6*
UNION 76 ADVERTISING (m.c.)	*$1–$3*

WATER TRANSPORTATION VALUES

American Line (e.c., adv)	*$8–$15*
BATTLESHIPS (e.c.)	*$3–$20*
BATTLESHIPS (m.c.)	*$1–$10*
BATTLESHIPS (l.c.)	*$1–$3*
CANAL BOATS	*$2–$20*
Celebrated Liners, p/Tuck	*$12–$18*
COAST GUARD	*$2–$20*
COASTAL STEAMERS (adv)	*$3–$15*
CUNARD LINE	*$3–$35*
EMBROIDERED SILK	*$50–$150*

Courtesy of Fred Schiffman

WOVEN IN SILK.

R.M.S. CARONIA.

21,000 tons.   676 feet long.   72 feet 6 inches broad.

Embroidered silk of the RMS Caronia. Scarce. Value: $60.

Empire Series, p/Tuck $20–$25

Courtesy of Fred Schiffman

The HMS Victory, #254 *from Raphael Tuck & Sons's Empire Series. Not common.* Value: $20.

FERRIES (e.c.)	$3–$20
Real photo	$8–$40
FERRIES (m.c.)	$2–$10
FERRIES (l.c.)	$1–$3
GREAT WHITE FLEET (pio., e.c.)	$10–$150
p/American Souvenir Card	$25–$30
Uncle Sam's Warships, accordion fold	
	$150
LIGHTHOUSES (e.c.)	$2–$15
LIGHTHOUSES (m.c.)	$1–$10
LIGHTHOUSES (l.c.)	$1–$3
NYK LINE	$15–$20

From the author's collection

Artist-drawn with gold highlights, with an inset of the NYK line's SS Nikko Maru. *Not common.* Value: $15.

OCEANLINERS (pio.), p/American Souvenir Card	
	$25–$35
OCEANLINERS (e.c.)	$3–$10
Real photo	$5–$15
OCEANLINERS (m.c.)	$2–$10
OCEANLINERS (l.c.)	$1–$6
Pacific Mail (e.c., adv)	$6–$15
RED STAR LINE	$3–$40
RIVER BOATS (e.c.)	$2–$10
Real photo	$7–$20

Courtesy of Joel Edler

Real photo view: waiting for the riverboat Pauline on the Mississippi River. Postally used 1913. Scarce. Value: $30.

RIVER BOATS (m.c.)	$1–$4
RIVER BOATS (l.c.)	$1–$3
SAILBOATS	$2–$20

Courtesy of John and Sandy Millns

Private mailing card of the Columbia, the America's Cup defender, 1898. Scarce. Value: $30.

SAILING SHIPS (e.c.)	$2–$20
SAILING SHIPS (m.c.)	$1–$10
SAILING SHIPS (l.c.)	$1–$3
SUBMARINES	$2–$20
TITANIC	$20–$100

Courtesy of John and Sandy Millns

Photo view of the Titanic, *published by Beagles Postcards; a credit on the photo reads "Central News." There is much competition for* Titanic *postcards.* Value: $60.

Courtesy of John and Sandy Millns

This view shows the Titanic *and the* Olympic *under construction. The* Titanic *is on the left. A rare postcard.* Value: $75.

Remember! All prices in this guide represent postcards in *Excellent* condition.

THE ILL-FATED S. S. TITANIC. FOUNDERED APRIL 15, 1912

*Artist-drawn postcard described as "The Ill-fated SS Titanic . . ."
—this is really the Olympic! After it sank, there was great demand
for Titanic postcards, but there was no Titanic to photograph! The
Olympic, without an enclosed deck forward, was used as a
close substitute. (The Titanic's upper deck was enclosed forward.)* Value: $40.

TUGBOATS   *$1–$8*

> *The minimum value in this price guide is $1. While many
> dealers offer 25-cent and 50-cent "bargain boxes," few
> dealers sort, individually price, and protectively "sleeve"
> postcards valued at less than $1. This price guide offers
> values for postcards worth $1 or more.*

Appendix

Major Postcard Publishers and Printers

The following lists the major publishers, printers, and distributors of postcards, including the period of production and representative work.

A. & S. (e.c.) St. Patricks, Thanksgiving, and religious greetings.

A.S.B. (e.c.) Decoration Day, Thanksgiving, Santa, Easter, and religious greetings.

ACKERMANN. (pio.) New York City views.

ACMEGRAPH COMPANY. (e.c.) Chicago publisher of views and comic romance.

AD/ART PHOTO SERVICE. (l.c.) Williamsport, Pennsylvania, distributor of regional views.

ADAMS, S. G. (e.c.) St. Louis stationer, publisher of a 1904 World's Fair series.

AERIAL PHOTOGRAPHY SERVICES, INC. (l.c.) Atlanta, Georgia, distributor of regional views in south Atlantic states.

ALBERTYPE COMPANY, BROOKLYN, NEW YORK. (1867–1952) Publisher of pioneer views; printer of Trans-Mississippi (1898), Pan-American (1901), Saratoga, New York, Floral Fete and Carnival (1901), South Carolina Inter-State (1902), St. Louis (1904), Panama-Pacific (1915), and Panama-California (1915) expo views; and publisher/printer of U.S. small-town views, many hand colored.

ALLLENTOWN ADPOSTAL CORPORATION. Pennsylvania, publisher of advertisements on government postal cards (1911–1913).

AMERICAN COLORTYPE. (e.c.) Chicago and New York printer of St. Louis expo (1904) views for Samuel Cupples, V. O. Hammon, and "Souvenirs of Jerusalem"; Jamestown expo views for Jamestown Amusement and Vending Company; and World War I views of American soldiers.

AMERICAN LITHOGRAPHIC COMPANY. (pio. and e.c.) Printer for Charles W. Goldsmith of official souvenir views of Columbian expo (1893); private mailing cards of oceanliners for the American Line; advertising postcards for Rumford Baking Powder; and comic advertising cards of stoves.

AMERICAN NEWS COMPANY. (e.c.) Publisher of "litho-chrome" (printed in Germany) views of the Panama Canal construction; distributor of "Excelsior" and "Poly-Chrome" local U.S. views (printed in Germany).

AMERICAN POST CARD COMPANY. (e.c.) New York publisher of designs by English artist Amy Millicent Sowerby.

AMERICAN POST CARD COMPANY, SEATTLE. (e.c.) Publisher of souvenir views for Alaska-Yukon-Pacific expo (1909).

AMERICAN POST CARD COMPANY. (l.c.) New York publisher of contemporary humor and topicals.

AMERICAN SOUVENIR CARD COMPANY. (1897–1898) Publisher of U.S. pioneer view cards and U.S. war ships.

AMERICAN SOUVENIR COMPANY. (pio.) Boston publisher of views of Boston (1895–1896).

ANGLO-AMERICAN POST CARD COMPANY. (e.c.) Publisher of Halloween and Thanksgiving greetings; Hudson Fulton celebration (1909); "Our Merry Widow" days of the week series; and "Open Book" series 726 and 727 (Lincoln) and 725 and 728 (Washington).

ARAM. (e.c.) Publisher of photocards of Harvard-Boston Flying Meet (1910).

ARCADE VIEW COMPANY. (e.c.) Publisher of Panama-California expo views (1915).

ARCTIC CIRCLE ENTERPRISES, INC. (l.c.) Anchorage, Alaska, distributor of regional views.

ARGUS COMMUNICATIONS. (l.c.) Allen, Texas, publisher of Garfield postcards.

ARKANSAS POST CARD COMPANY. (l.c.) North Little Rock, Arkansas, distributor of regional views.

ARMOUR AND COMPANY. (e.c.) Publisher of "American Girl" series of drawings by famous illustrators (ca. 1905).

ARMSTRONG AND COMPANY. (pio.) Printer for American Souvenir Company of views of Boston (1895–1896).

ART LITHO. COMPANY. (e.c.) A printing subsidiary of Edward H. Mitchell Company of San Francisco.

ART UNLIMITED. (l.c.) Holland, publisher of black-and-white and color photographic topicals.

ARTINO COMPANY. (e.c.) Issued for E. F. Branning; a scarce set of Sunbonnet Babies postcards.

ARTS AND CARDS. (l.c.) Brookline, Massachusetts, distributor of regional views.

ASHEVILLE POST CARD CO. (m.c.) Asheville, North Carolina, publisher of U.S. views.

ASTROCARD. (l.c.) Staford, Texas, distributor of regional views.

ATHENA. (l.c.) English publisher of artist-drawn and photographic topicals.

AUBURN POST CARD MANUFACTURING CO. (e.c.) Auburn, Indiana, publisher of patriotics, comics, greetings, World War I military and battleships.

AUSTIN, J. I. (e.c.) Publisher of topical series of famous Americans; two travel series; "Busy Bears" day of the week series; a college girl series drawn by Bernhardt Wall; and a Sunbonnet series by Bertha Corbett.

AVERY POSTCARDS. (l.c.) Wichita, Kansas, distributor of regional views.

AVIL, J. H. (e.c.) Publisher of private mailing card series with flag and eagle.

AZUZA. (l.c.) Denver, Colorado, publisher of Indian and historical topicals.

BAMFORTH COMPANY. (e.c., m.c.) British publisher of comics and romance; also series issued in United States, including hymns, World War I, and temperance comics and other comments on fads, fashion, and behavior.

BARDELL ART PRINTING COMPANY. (e.c.) Published an unofficial series for Panama-Pacific expo (1915).

BARTON AND SPOONER. (e.c.) Publisher of comic series on subjects including suffrage; Dutch children; Rube Goldberg's Foolish Questions; Glass House, and Inventions series; St. Patricks', patriotic, Halloween, and Thanksgiving greetings.

BECK, CHARLES A. (e.c.) Publisher of designs of Miss Liberty on Fourth of July greetings (1908).

BEHRENDT, RICHARD. (e.c.) San Francisco publisher of cards for Panama-Pacific expo (1915) and San Francisco earthquake.

BERGMAN COMPANY. (e.c.) Publisher of suffrage comics and Sunbonnet Babies drawn by Bernhardt Wall.

BERGMAN, JOHN. (e.c.) Copyrighted series of college girls (1905).

BIEN, JULIUS. (e.c.) Printer of campaign, comic, college girl, and July 4th, Lincoln and Halloween greetings.

BILLINGS NEWS, INC. (l.c.) Billings, Montana, distributor of regional views.

BIRN BROTHERS. (e.c.) British publisher of comic political cards.

BLAU, CHARLES J. (pio.) Pioneer view publisher.

BOSSELMAN, A. C., AND COMPANY. (e.c.) Prolific U.S. view card publisher, also noted for Jamestown expo (1907) views, Taft views, movie industry, and state capitols.

BRAENDLE, FRED. (e.c.) Publisher of campaign postcards for 1900 election.

BRANNING, E. F. (e.c.) Of Artino Company of New York. Issued private mailing card views with colored emblems of Miss Liberty and a scarce Sunbonnet Babies series.

BRITTON AND REY. (e.c.) San Francisco lithographers, published views and St. Louis expo (1904), Portola Festival officials (1909), Panama-Pacific expo (1915), Great White Fleet, San Francisco earthquake cards.

BRYANT UNION. (e.c.) New York City publisher of historical topics.

BURBANK, A. S. (pio., e.c.) Plymouth, Massachusetts, view card publisher (printed by Detroit Publishing Company).

BUSCH, F. A. (e.c.) Publisher of unofficial views of Pan-American expo (1901).

BUXTON AND SKINNER. (e.c.) Publisher of silver background views of St. Louis expo (1904).

CAMPBELL ART COMPANY. (e.c.) Elizabeth, New Jersey, publisher of Rose O'Neil kewpie "Klever Kards" (1914).

CAPPER, ARTHUR. (e.c.) Topeka, Kansas, publisher of "Roosevelt Tour" series (1909).

CARDINELL-VINCENT. (e.c.) Subsidiary of Edward H. Mitchell of San Francisco; official publisher for Panama-Pacific expo (1915), also San Francisco earthquake views.

CARDS UNLIMITED. (l.c.) Keysville, Virginia, distributor of regional views.

CARGILL COMPANY. (e.c.) Grand Rapids, Michigan, publisher of a suffrage series (1910).

CARSON-HARPER. (pio., e.c.) Denver publisher of pioneer views and private mailing cards of Indians.

CARTWHEEL COMPANY. (l.c.) St. Paul, Minnesota, distributor of regional views.

CHARLTON, E. P. (e.c.) Publisher of unofficial Lewis & Clark expo (1905), Alaska-Yukon-Pacific expo (1907), views of San Francisco earthquake, other views printed by E. H. Mitchell.

CHICAGO COLORTYPE COMPANY. (pio.) Engraver/printer for 1898 U.S. Postal Card Company's official Trans-Mississippi expo views.

CHISHOLM BROTHERS. (pio., e.c.) Portland, Maine, lithographers of pioneer views, St. Louis expo (1904) views, and New England views.

CHRUCHMAN COMPANY. (e.c.) New York publisher of Hudson-Fulton celebration views (1909).

CLASSICO SAN FRANCISCO. (l.c.) San Rafael, California, publisher/printer of movie stars, movie stills, Norman Rockwell, Betty Boop.

CLEVELAND NEWS COMPANY. (e.c.) Published series of presidential portraits.

COLDEWEY, GEORGE. (e.c.) Springfield, Illinois, view card publisher plus series for St. Louis World's Fair (1904).

COLORTYPE COMPANY. (pio.) New York City printer of American Souvenir Card Company's views.

COLOURPICTURE. (m.c.) Boston, Massachusetts, printer/publisher of U.S. views.

COMMERCIAL COLORTYPE COMPANY. (e.c.) Publisher of Ford Motor Company comic ads drawn by Cobb X. Shinn; Sheridan's Ride series.

CONWELL, L. R. (e.c.) New York publisher of Halloween and patriotic greetings, copyrighter of Maud Humphrey designs.

COOK, L. L. (m.c.) Milwaukee, Wisconsin, printer/publisher of real photo, linen, and chrome views of the Midwest; acquired E. C. Kropp Company in 1956.

CORAL-LEE. (l.c.) Rancho Cordova, California, publisher of contemporary topicals and dated events.

CROCKER, H. S. (e.c., m.c., l.c.) San Francisco, California, publisher/printer of U.S. view cards.

CROWN GREETINGS. (m.c., l.c.) Cleveland, Ohio, distributor of regional views.

CUPPLES, SAMUEL, ENVELOPE COMPANY. (e.c.) Official publisher of St. Louis expo (1904) cards; hold-to-light views.

DAY, BENJAMIN. (e.c.) New York printer, invented "Ben Day" process of varying size and density of color dots to achieve shading effect.

DEDERICK BROTHERS. (e.c.) Published elongated letter puzzle series of novelty postcards (1906–1907).

DETROIT PUBLISHING COMPANY. (1888–1932) Detroit, Michigan, printer/publisher of U.S., Canada, Mexico, and West Indies views including two-and three-panel panoramic views, plus Hudson-Fulton celebration (1909), Panama-Pacific expo (1915), Panama-California expo (1915), and Mardi Gras; newspaper, railroad, and steamship advertising postcards; infantry and naval scenes; American Indians and other ethnic groups; river and great lakes shipping; industry and agriculture; performers;

amusement attractions; famous people and events; and miscellaneous arts including smokes, drinks, mermaid, butterfly girls, childhood days, gnomes, and international girls sets by Samuel L. Schmucker; cartoons from "Life" by Charles Dana Gibson; work of John Cecil Clay, Harrison Fisher, Peter Newell, William Balfour Ker, Bayard Jones, and Frederick Remington.

DEXTER PRESS. (m.c., l.c.) Printer/publisher of U.S. views.

DICKSON, G. R., COMPANY. (l.c.) Denver, Colorado, distributor of regional views.

DOUGLAS, MRS. HOWARD GRAY. (e.c.) Publisher of Washington, Arlington, and Mt. Vernon views printed by Photo Electric Engraving Company of New York.

DOVER PUBLICATIONS, INC. (l.c.) Mineola, New York, publisher of topicals and reproductions.

DUNLAP POSTCARD COMPANY. (l.c.) Omaha, Nebraska, distributor of regional views.

DUSTON-WEILER LITHOGRAPHIC COMPANY. (e.c.) Dunkirk, New York, publisher of satiric suffrage series.

EASTERN ILLUSTRATING COMPANY. (l.c.) Union, Maine, distributor of Vermont-New Hampshire views.

EDWARDS PRESS. (l.c.) Rochester, New York, distributor of regional views.

ELKUS, EDWARD. (e.c.) Publisher of Great White Fleet welcome card.

EMPIRE P. AND P. COMPANY. (e.c.) Publisher of Hudson-Fulton celebration (1909) views.

ENO, I. L. (e.c.) Publisher of Panama–California expo views printed by Curt Teich.

ENVIRONMENTAL PHOTOART. (l.c.) Pelham, Alabama, distributor of regional views.

EXPOSITION PUBLISHING COMPANY. (e.c.) Publishers of pre-expo cards for Panama-Pacific expo.

FAULKNER. (e.c.) British publisher of Shakespeare designs by Kyd, distributed in United States by Osborne.

FERLONI, A. (e.c.) Rome, Italy, publisher of Illuminated Papal series.

FINKENRATH, PAUL (P.F.B.) (e.c.) Berlin publisher of artist-drawn holiday greetings and topicals including religious, comic family, and children; Lincoln centennial, Valentine's Day, Fourth of July, Halloween, Thanksgiving, and Christmas greetings.

FOTOFOLIO. (l.c.) New York publisher of photo art postcards.

GABRIEL, SAM. (e.c.) American publisher of Halloween and Thanksgiving greetings; unsigned Francis Brundage Decoration Day and Saint Patrick's Day greetings, DWIG designs.

GERMAN-AMERICAN NOVELTY ART COMPANY. (e.c.) Distributor of greetings with animals, flowers, elves, and Japanese, Thanksgiving, and birth announcement subjects.

GIBSON ART COMPANY. (e.c.) Publisher of Bernhardt Wall and Rosie O'Neil designs.

GIES AND COMPANY. (e.c.) Buffalo, New York, lithographer of Pan-American expo cards (1901).

GLAZER, LOUIS. (pio., e.c.) Leipzig, Germany, lithographer.

GOEGGEL AND WEIDNER. (e.c.) San Francisco view card publisher.

GOIN COMPANY. (m.c., l.c.) Mitchell, South Dakota, distributor of regional views, Corn Palace.

GOLDSMITH, CHARLES W. (pio.) Distributor for official Columbian expo (1893) souvenir postal cards.

GOTTSCHALK, DREYFUSS AND DAVIS. (e.c.) Publisher of George Washington, July Fourth, Halloween, and Thanksgiving greetings.

GRAFF, BERNHARD M. (e.c.) Publisher of St. Louis World's Fair (1904) series with private mailing card back.

GREAT MOUNTAIN WEST SUPPLY, INC. (l.c.) Salt Lake City, Utah, distributor of regional views.

GRIMM, E. A. AND COMPANY. (pio.) Hamburg, Germany, publisher of Philadelphia pioneers.

GROLLMAN, I. (e.c.) Publisher of comic greetings and topicals including political, "Merry Widow Hat" (1908), and Leap Year series.

GROSS, EDWARD. (e.c.) New York publisher, copyrighter of Pearle Eugenia Fidler designs.

GULF STREAM CARD AND DISTRIBUTING COMPANY, INC. (m.c., l.c.) Miami, Florida, distributor of regional views.

H.S.V. LITHOGRAPH COMPANY. (e.c.) Printer of Billy Possum designs copyrighted by L. Gulick (1909); New Year's series by DWIG; Thanksgiving greetings.

HAGELBERG, W. (e.c.) Publisher of early hold-to-lights.

HAHN, ALBERT, COMPANY. (e.c.) Publisher of Eugene Debs campaign card.

HAMMON, V. O. (e.c.) Minneapolis and Chicago publisher of views of major Midwest cities, St. Louis expo (1904), perforated novelty cards.

HARRIS, GEORGE S. AND SONS. (pio.) New York printer of pioneer views of Philadelphia.

HARVEY, FRED. (e.c.) Hotel/restaurant chain publisher of American Indians and views of Southwest, contract printed by Detroit Publishing Company.

HASPELMETH, CHARLES. (pio.) Santa Fe, New Mexico, pioneer view publisher.

HAYNES PHOTO COMPANY. (e.c., m.c.) Publisher of views of Yellowstone National Park.

HEAL, WILLIAM S. (e.c.) Publisher of teddy bear days of the week (1907), and novelty postcards including padded silk pincushions, real shells, and a "Magic Post Card Match Scratcher."

HEARST NEWSPAPERS. (e.c.) Publisher of sheets of postcard views, comics (by artists Frederick Burr Opper, Richard Felton Outcault), and San Francisco earthquake as supplements in Sunday newspapers.

HENDERSON, JAMES, AND SONS. (e.c.) British publisher/distributor of Gibson girl postcards.

HENDERSON LITHOGRAPHING COMPANY. (e.c.) Cincinnati, Ohio, publisher of Gound Hog's Day greetings.

HESSE ENVELOPE COMPANY. (e.c.) Distributor of St. Louis expo (1904) views.

HILL, RUFUS. (e.c.) Member of publishing firm Edward Stern and Company; copyrighter of college girl designs and "Roller Skating" set drawn by George Reiter Brill.

HINDE, JOHN, CURTEICH. (l.c.) Ireland printer of U.S. views.

HOLBROOK, GEORGE F. (e.c.) Publisher of child's prayer series.

HOLLANDER, JOSEPH. (e.c.) Publisher of pre-expo issue (1906) for Jamestown expo (1907).

HOLLISTER, GEORGE K. (pio.) New York City pioneer publisher of cards with actual photo attachments.

HOLZMAN, ALFRED. (e.c.) Chicago publisher of views.

HOPF BROTHERS. (e.c.) Publisher of Alaska-Yukon-Pacific expo (1909) cards.

HOPF, JOHN T., PHOTOGRAPHY. (l.c.) Newport, Rhode Island, distributor of regional views.

HORNE, W.H., COMPANY. (e.c.) El Paso, Texas, publisher of real photo views of Mexican border war.

HULD, FRANZ. (e.c.) New York view and topical publisher plus Pan-American expo (1901), National Saengerfest (1903), and Hudson-Fulton celebration (1909) cards; McKinley commemorative, Roosevelt-Longworth wedding, and 1904 and 1908 presidential campaigns; Prince Henry's yacht (1902), Treaty of Portsmouth (1905) commemorative, San Francisco earthquake (1906); college girl, navy, historical, literary, and Wagner opera series, as well as novelty installment sets.

IEZZI, ANTHONY L. (l.c.) Laureldale, Pennsylvania, distributor of regional views.

ILLUSTRATED POSTAL CARD COMPANY. (e.c.) Publisher of New York views and also of Jamestown (1907), Philadelphia's Founder's Week (1908), and Hudson-Fulton (1909) commemoratives; World War I patriotics, Coney Island views; presidential and state capitols series; religious, dressed bears, college girl, character/occupations subjects; and work by F. Earl Christy, Archie Gunn, Harry Hershfield, August William Hutaf, Paul de Longpre, and Bernhardt Wall; birth announcement, Christmas and Uncle Sam greetings; and silk appliqué and hold-to-light novelty cards.

IMPACT. (l.c.) Publisher/distributor of U.S. views and topicals.

INDIAN ARTS & CRAFTS, INC. (l.c.) Seattle, Washington, distributor of regional views.

INTERNATIONAL ART COMPANY. (e.c.) New York publisher of designs by George J. Beck, Ellen H. Clapsaddle, Cyrus Durand Chapman, Magnus Greiner, Ana Alberta Heinmuller, Richard Veenfliet, and Bernhardt Wall; embossed patriotics and greetings for New Year's, Lincoln's, and Washington's Birthdays, Valentine's, St. Patrick's Day, Easter, Fourth of July, Halloween, Thanksgiving and Christmas; and novelty mechanicals.

ISLAND CURIO. (e.c.) Honolulu publisher of views and a colorful series of Hawaiian fish.

J & H SALES COMPANY, INC. (l.c.) Portland, Oregon, distributor of regional views.

JACKSON, WILLIAM HENRY. (e.c.) Photographer and part-owner of Detroit Publishing Company.

JAMESTOWN AMUSEMENT AND VENDING COMPANY. (e.c.) Publisher of offical views for Jamestown expo (1907).

JOHNSTON-AYRES COMPANY. (e.c.) Copyrighter of zodiac postcard set printed by Edward H. Mitchell.

JOHNSTON, J. S. (pio.) Publisher of pioneer hold-to-light views.

KANSAS POSTCARD COMPANY. (l.c.) Lawrence, Kansas, distributor of regional views.

KAPLAN, R. (e.c.) Publisher of comic "Jungle Lovers" series and designs by DWIG.

KAUFMAN AND STRAUS. (e.c.) Publisher of comic advertising cards for Holsum Bread and Fred Opper's Happy Hooligan on Valentine's greetings.

KAWIN AND COMPANY. (e.c.) Chicago publisher of series for return of Roosevelt Tour (1910) and of Cook and Peary North Pole expeditions.

KAYSER, A. (pio.) Oakland, California, publisher of San Francisco area pioneer views.

KENYON, BREWSTER C. (pio.) Long Beach, California, publisher of Columbian Exposition-related issue.

KINA ITALIA. (l.c.) Italian printer of postcard views.

KLEIN POSTCARD SERVICE. (l.c.) Boston, Massachusetts, distributor of regional views.

KOEBER, PAUL C. (e.c.) Publisher of a 1908 Leap Year series and 1909 April Fool designs by August Hutaf.

KOEHLER, JOSEPH. (pio., e.c.) New York publisher of U.S. views, private mailing cards, and die-cut, hold-to-light views; plus unofficial Columbian expo (1893), St. Louis expo (1904), Hudson-Fulton celebration (1909), and Mardi Gras carnival issues; and commemoratives of Prince Henry's yacht, Cook's discovery of North Pole, Uncle Sam and John Bull; plus rare novelty pop-up designs.

KOELLING AND KLAPPENBACK. (e.c.) Chicago publisher of views and commemoratives.

KOHLE, HERMAN. (pio.) Brunswick, New Jersey, publisher of New York City pioneer views.

KOLB BROTHERS. (e.c.) Publisher of views of Grand Canyon.

KREH, C. F. TH. (pio., e.c.) New York City pioneer publisher.

KROPP, E.C. (1896–1956) Milwaukee, Wisconsin, view card printer/publisher including pioneer issues of warships, Milwaukee, Detroit, and Chicago; McKinley commemorative and private mailing card views; unofficial St. Louis expo (1904) issues; American Indians, rare state capitols set; printer for Bryant Union; and printer of Alaska-Yukon-Pacific expo issues for Portland Post Card Company.

LAMERTIN, A. (e.c.) Toronto publisher including views of Pan-American expo (1901).

LANGE AND SCHWALBACK. (e.c.) American view card publisher including Colonial Heroes series, shell-border and shell-frame views.

LANGSDORF, SAMUEL. (e.c.) Publisher of alligator-border scenes of the South and shell-border views of the Atlantic coast; embossed state capitols set; military and naval uniforms series and battleships; air-brush designs for Hudson-Fulton celebration (1909), Easter greetings, Santas, state belles, cowgirls, and college girls both with and without silk appliqué; and Easter and Thanksgiving greetings.

LEET BROTHERS. (e.c.) Published views of 1913 suffrage parade.

LEIGHTON, HUGH C. (e.c.) Portland, Maine, publisher of U. S. views;

in 1910 joined with Valentine & Sons of New York and Dundee, Scotland; published state capitols series; reprinted set of Tuck presidents.

LEUBRIE AND ELKUS. (e.c.) Published work by artists H. B. Griggs, Gertrude L. Pew, M. Quarls, and Mary La Fenetra Russell.

LIPMAN, H.L. (pio.) Published, privately printed mailing card, "Lipman's Postal Card" in 1869, pre-dating U.S. government postal cards.

LIVINGSTON, ARTHUR. (pio., e.c.) New York publisher of pioneer and later U.S. views; 1901 Pan-American expo views, and Vinegar Valentines.

LONDON AND SUBURBAN PHOTOGRAPHIC COMPANY. (e.c.) British view card printer.

LOUNSBURY, FRED C. (e.c.) U.S. view and topical publisher including Hudson-Fulton celebration views, 1908 Philadelphia Founder's Week commemorative, and Billy Possum cards celebrating Taft's victory; fortune series; and Lincoln, Decoration Day, Fourth of July, Labor Day, Halloween, and Thanksgiving greetings.

LOWEY, EDWARD. (pio.) New York City pioneer view card publisher.

LOWMAN AND HANFORD (e.c.) Seattle view card publisher including Lewis and Clark expo (1905) and Alaska-Yukon-Pacific (1909) views.

LUDLOW SALES. (l.c.) New York publisher of movie stars.

MacFARLANE, W.G. (e.c.) Toronto publisher of views, and St. Louis (1904) and Lewis & Clark (1905) expo issues.

McINTOSH, BURR. (e.c.) Publisher of Buster Brown and his Bubble designs.

McLAUGHLIN BROTHERS. (e.c.) Publisher of Vinegar Valentines.

MADURO, J. L. (e.c., m.c.) Photographer/publisher of Panama Canal views.

MAGEE AND ROBINSON. (e.c.) Printer of pre-expo issue for Jamestown expo.

MAGEE ART COMPANY. (e.c.) Philadelphia publisher of dressed kittens days of the week series (1906).

MAINE SCENE. (l.c.) Union, Maine, distributor of regional views.

MAINZER, ALFRED, INC. (m.c., l.c.) Long Island City, New York, publisher of dressed cats, topicals, and regional views.

MANHATTAN POST CARD COMPANY, INC. (m.c., l.c.) Glendale, New York, publisher of exposition views, topicals, and regional views.

MARKS, J. J. (e.c.) Publisher of greetings.

MARY JAYNE'S RAILROAD SPECIALTIES INC. (l.c.) Covington, Virginia, publisher of transportation subjects.

MATTHEWS NORTHRUP (pio.) Buffalo, New York, publisher/printer of pioneer views of Buffalo; advertising folder postcard for Inside Inn at Jamestown expo (1907).

MEDICI SOCIETY, LTD. (m.c.) London, England, publisher of nursery rhymes, artist signed (Brett Ward, Racey Helps, Margaret W. Tarrant.)

MEISSNER & BUCH. (e.c.) Publisher/printer quality greetings.

MERCHANTS POST CARD COMPANY. (e.c.) Publisher of Halloween greetings.

METROCRAFT CO. (m.c.) Everett, Massachusetts, publisher of views and comics.

METROPOLITAN NEWS COMPANY. (e.c.) Publisher of U.S. views.

MITCHELL, EDWARD H., COMPANY. (1898–1915) U.S. west coast view card printer/publisher, and also expo views for Lewis and Clark (1905), Alaska-Yukon-Pacific (1909), Panama-Pacific (1915), and Panama-California (1915); Portola Festival (1909); and American Indians, Chinese, exaggerated fruit, battleships, and zodiac subjects.

MITOCK PUBLISHERS, INC. (l.c.) North Hollywood, California, distributor of local views.

MOFFAT, YARD, AND COMPANY. (e.c.) Publisher of Howard Chandler Christy designs.

MOORE AND GIBSON. (e.c.) New York publisher of comic subjects.

MORRIS, G. W. (e.c.) Portland, Maine, publisher of U.S. view cards.

MOUNTAIN STATES SPECIALTIES, INC. (l.c.) Boulder, Colorado, distributor of regional views.

MUNK, MAX. (e.c.) Printing firm in Vienna, Austria, produced some "Miscellaneous Arts" cards for Detroit Publishing Company.

NASH, E. (e.c.) U.S. publisher of greetings and topics including birth announcements, birthday, Lincoln's Birthday, Valentine's Day, Washington's Birthday, Leap Year, St. Patrick's Day, Decoration Day, Fourth of July, Labor Day, Halloween, and Thanksgiving greetings.

NATIONAL ART COMPANY. (e.c.) Publisher of topicals including nursery rhymes, state girls series, and artist-signed Katherine Gassaway designs.

NISTER, ERNEST. (1902–1927) British publisher of greetings and topics including Shakespearian characters and artist signed (Ethel DeWees, Albertine Randall Wheelan, C. E. Brock, Louis Wain)

NORTHERN MINNESOTA NOVELTIES. (l.c.) Crosslake, Minnesota, distributor of regional views.

NUGERON. (l.c.) French publisher of topicals.

NU-VISTA PRINTS. (l.c.) Willowick, Ohio, distributor of regional views.

OLDROYD, O. H. (e.c.) Publisher of Lincoln souvenir cards.

OSBORNE COMPANY.(e.c.) New York distributor of Faulkner's Dickens designs by KYD and Ethel Parkinson's children designs.

OTTENHEIMER, I. & M. (e.c.) Baltimore view card publisher including Taft and Wilson inaugurations, and photocards of woman suffrage march (1913) and other events.

OUT OF THE WEST PUBLISHING. (l.c.) Sacramento, California, publisher of topicals including fruit crate labels and automobile posters.

OWEN, F. A. (e.c.) Publisher of greetings and topicals including work by artist Florence England Nosworthy.

P. F. B. *See* Finkenrath, Paul.

PACIFIC NOVELTY COMPANY. (e.c.) San Francisco subsidiary of Edward Mitchell, publisher of views, San Francisco earthquake, and Portola Festival poster-style cards.

PAIGE CREATIONS. (l.c.) Morgantown, West Virginia, distributor of regional views.

PENDOR NATURAL COLOR. (l.c.) Pearl River, New York, distributor of regional views.

PENROD/HIAWATHA CARD COMPANY. (l.c.) Berrien Center, Michigan, distributor of regional views.

PETLEY STUDIOS, INC. (m.c., l.c.) Phoenix, Arizona, distributor of regional views and comics.

PHORO-COLOR-GRAPH. (e.c.) New York greetings and patriotics publisher.

PHOTO ELECTRIC ENGRAVING COMPANY. (e.c.) New York printer of quality similar to Detroit Publishing Company.

PINKAU, EMIL. (e.c.) Leipzig printer of private mailing cards, views, and exposition issues.

PITT SOUVENIRS. (l.c.) Northbrook, Illinois, distributor of regional views.

PLATINACHROME. (e.c.) Publisher of topicals including state girls, national belles, and Christy college girls.

POMEGRANATE. (l.c.) Petaluma, California, publisher of topicals.

PORTLAND POST CARD COMPANY. (e.c.) Publisher of official views for Alaska-Yukon-Pacific expo (1909).

PRANG, LOUIS. (pio., e.c.) Roxbury, Massachusetts, publisher of Christmas (non-postcard) greetings; renamed Taber-Prang Art Company when Prang retired in 1897, issued private mailing cards of Boston area.

PRINCE, L. B. (l.c.) Fairfax, Virginia, distributor of regional views.

QUANTITY POSTCARDS. (l.c.) San Francisco, California, publisher of contemporary topicals.

REDFIELD BROTHERS, INC. (e.c.) New York City publisher and official publisher for Hudson-Fulton celebration (1909).

REGENSTEINER COLORTYPE. (e.c.) Chicago printer, including Portland Post Card Company's Alaska-Yukon-Pacific official expo cards.

REICHNER BROTHERS. (e.c.) Boston publisher of luminous window cards.

REID, ROBERT A. (e.c.) Seattle view card publisher including official photoviews of Alaska-Yukon-Pacific (1909).

REINTHAL AND NEWMAN. (e.c.) New York topical publisher including political, greetings, and children; artist-signed designs by Philip Boileau, F. Earl Christy, Harrison Fisher, Raphael Kirchner, Amy Millicent Sowerby, Clarence F. Underwood, and Grace Wiederseim.

RENO-TAHOE SPECIALTY, INC. (l.c.) Tahoe City, California, distributor of regional views.

RICH, B. B. (e.c.) Portland view card publisher and official cards for Lewis & Clark expo (1905).

RIEDER, M. (e.c.) Los Angeles view publisher, most printed by Edward Mitchell, and topicals including American Indians, San Francisco earthquake.

RIGOT, MAX (e.c., m.c.) Chicago publisher of local views and events, topicals, and novelties.

ROBERTS, MIKE. (m.c., l.c.) Oakland, California, publisher/printer of U.S. views.

ROBBINS. (e.c.) Boston publisher of Sunbonnet Babies series.

ROSE, CHARLES. (e.c.) Published song series, artist-signed DWIG series.

ROSE COMPANY. (e.c.) Philadelphia publisher of historical educational series, Ten Commandments, Vinegar Valentines, Brill "Ginks," and installment novelties.

ROSE, H. M. (e.c.) Publisher of topicals including 1908 Philadelphia Founder's Week, and 1909 Hudson-Fulton celebration issues and North Pole comics.

ROSENBLATT. (e.c.) Frankfurt, Germany, lithographer produced high-quality views with artwork borders for local American distributors.

ROST, ERNST. (pio.) Pioneer view card publisher.

ROST, H. A. PRINTING AND PUBLISHING COMPANY. (pio.) Pioneer view card publisher.

ROTH & LANGLEY. (e.c.) New York publisher of sepia comics with real models.

ROTOGRAPH. (e.c.) U.S. views and topical publisher including expo/events (1904 St. Louis and Mardi Gras), advertising (Simplex cream separator and Burke's Guinness stout), battleships, college girls, disasters, ethnic, entertainers, fraternal, novelty cards, personalities/political (Roosevelt family, Treaty of Portsmouth, North Pole exploration, presidents), religious, Vinegar Valentines, and artist signed (Gene Carr, John Cecil Clay, Katherine Gassaway, and Paul de Longpre).

RUSHMORE NEWS, INC. (l.c.) Rapid City, South Dakota, distributor of regional views.

RUSHMORE PHOTO. (l.c.) Rapid City, South Dakota, distributor of regional views.

SACKETT AND WILHELMS. (e.c.) Brooklyn printing firm that merged with Hugh Leighton in 1910.

SANBORN SOUVENIR COMPANY, INC. (m.c., l.c.) Commerce City, Colorado, distributor of regional views.

SANDER, P. (e.c.) Topical and greetings publisher including artist signed (F. Earl Christy, August Hutaf, and Bernhardt Wall); greetings (birth announcements, Lincoln's and Washington's Birthdays, Leap Year, Easter, Fourth of July, Halloween, Thanksgiving, and Christmas Santas); humor, Lord's Prayer, Philadelphia Founder's Week, political, and novelty silk attachments.

SANTWAY. (e.c.) Publisher of holiday greetings (Decoration Day, Memorial Day, Fourth of July, Halloween, and Thanksgiving).

SBORGI, E. (e.c.) Florence, Italy, publisher of gallery art cards.

SCHAEFER, W. R. (pio.) Publisher of pioneer view of Philadelphia.

SCHEFF, I. AND BROTHERS. (e.c.) View card publisher including San Francisco earthquake.

SCHWERDTFEGER, E. A. (e.c.) Publisher's subjects include religious and college girls.

SCOFIELD SOUVENIR AND POST CARD COMPANY. (l.c.) Menomenee Falls, Wisconsin, distributor of regional views.

SCOPE ENTERPRISES. (l.c.) Clovis, California, distributor of regional views.

SEAICH CARD AND SOUVENIR CORP. (l.c.) Salt Lake City, Utah, distributor of regional views.

SECKEL, M. (pio.) Publisher of pioneer New York City views.

SELIGE, ADOLPH. (e.c.) St. Louis view card publisher and topicals including St. Louis expo (1904), Lewis & Clark expo (1905), Mardi Gras, American Indians and famous people, and San Francisco earthquake.

SEMINOLE SOUVENIRS, INC. (m.c., l.c.) Seminole, Florida, distributor of regional views.

SHEAHAN, M. T. (e.c.) Boston view and topical publisher including historical, famous people, fortune, Lincoln, and "The Martyred Presidents."

SHELLMARK, INC. (l.c.) Hackettstown, New Jersey, distributor of regional views.

SILBERNE SALES, INC. (l.c.) Washington, DC, distributor of regional views.

SMITH NOVELTY COMPANY. (l.c.) San Francisco, California, distributor of regional views.

SMITH-SOUTHWESTERN, INC. (l.c.) Tempe, Arizona, distributor of regional views.

SMITH WESTERN COMPANY, INC. (l.c.) Tacoma, Washington, distributor of regional views.

SOUTHERN EMPIRE. (l.c.) San Diego, California, distributor of regional views.

SOUTHERN POST CARD COMPANY, INC. (l.c.) Goodlettsville, Tennessee, distributor of regional views.

SOUVENIR POSTAL CARD COMPANY, ALBANY, NEW YORK. (pio.) Publisher of pioneer views of Albany.

SOUVENIR POST CARD COMPANY. (e.c.) View card publisher plus advertising (shoes, soap), college girls, Confederate heroes, San Francisco earthquake, novelty reproducing cards, and birthday and Thanksgiving greetings.

SPEYER H. W. (e.c.) New York publisher of pro-German cards (1915).

STANDARD POSTAL SOUVENIR CARD COMPANY. (pio.) Publisher of pioneer New York City views.

STAR PRINTING. (pio.) Publisher of pioneer views of Terre Haute, Indiana.

STECHER LITHOGRAPH COMPANY. (e.c.) Rochester, New York, topical and greetings publisher including artist-signed designs of children by Margaret Evans Price, and C. Klein roses.

STEHLI (m.c., l.c.) Swiss publisher of topicals, animals, and flowers.

STEIN, MAX. (e.c., m.c.) Chicago printer/publisher.

STEL-MAR. (m.c.) Lancaster, Pennsylvania, distributor of regional views.

STENGEL. (e.c.) Dresden, Germany, publisher of art cards.

STERN, EDWARD. (e.c.) Philadelphia printer/publisher of topicals including college girls, Roosevelt bears, and Vinegar Valentines.

STEWARD & WOOLF. (e.c.) London publisher of topicals and comics.

STOKES, FREDERICK A. COMPANY. (e.c.) Topical publisher including artist-signed Charles R. Twelvetrees and Clarence F. Underwood.

STORER'S CARDS, INC. (l.c.) Tulsa, Oklahoma, distributor of regional views.

STRATTON, H. H. (e.c.) Chattanooga, Tennessee, topicals publisher including Great White Fleet.

STRAUSS, ARTHUR. (e.c.) New York publisher of view cards and special issues including 1900 presidential campaign, 1900 Hoboken pier fire, and 1901 Pan-American expo.

STRAUSS, FERDINAND AND COMPANY. (pio.) Publisher of New York City pioneer views.

STRAUSS AND McPHERSON. (pio.) Publisher of New York and Washington views.

STROEFER, THEODORE. See German American Novelty Art Company.

T. P. & COMPANY. (e.c.) Publisher of topicals and artist-signed designs including Cobb Shinn.

TABER-PRANG ART COMPANY. (e.c.) Successor to Louis Prang firm in 1897; issued mailing cards of Boston.

TAGGART. (e.c.) New York publisher of greetings and topicals including bathing beauties and religious and Lincoln, St. Patrick's Day, Decoration Day, Halloween, Thanksgiving, and general greetings.

TAMMEN, H. H. (e.c.) Denver view card publisher and special topics including R. Farrington Elwell designs, advertising (Great Northern Railway); Buster Brown; Lewis & Clark (1905) and Panama-Pacific (1815) expos; and Indians.

TEICH, CURT. (1897–1966) Chicago, Illinois, prolific printer/publisher/distributor of U.S. view cards.

TEXAS POSTCARD COMPANY. (l.c.) Plano, Texas, distributor of regional views.

TICHNOR BROTHERS. (e.c., m.c.) Boston-Los Angeles view card printer/publisher.

TUCK, RAPHAEL, AND SONS. (1866–World War II) Prolific British publisher of greetings, views, artist signed, and topicals extending from the pioneer period through World War II and covering all subjects imaginable from aviation, children, and comics to wildlife, women, and worldwide views.

ULLMAN MANUFACTURING CO. (e.c.) New York publisher of topicals and greetings including college girls, comics, dressed bears, North Pole exploration, political, suffrage, and Sunbonnet Babies; artist-signed Katherine Gassaway, Richard Outcault, and Bernhardt Wall; and "Pick the Pickaninnies" novelty.

UNION OIL COMPANY. (1939–1955) Publisher/distributor of U.S. views advertising product.

U.S. POSTAL CARD COMPANY. (e.c.) Omaha, Nebraska, publisher of official views for Trans-Mississippi expo (1898).

U.S. POST CARD COMPANY. (e.c.) Wilmington, Delaware, publisher of "the Official State Seal and Governor Post Card" set.

U.S.S.P. C. COMPANY. (e.c.) Publisher of topical sets including college girls, comic Shakespeare, and New England governors and state seals.

UNIVERSAL POSTAL CARD COMPANY. (pio.) New York publisher of pioneer views of New York and of the Spanish American War.

VALENTINE AND SONS. (e.c., m.c.) Prolific British publisher of greetings, comics, royalty, topicals, and artist signed (Barribal, Frank Feller, May Gladwin, and Louis Wain).

VOLLAND, P. F. AND COMPANY. (e.c.) Chicago, Illinois, publisher of topicals, greetings, and artist signed.

WAGNER, PAUL. (pio.) Publisher of pioneer view of San Antonio, Texas.

WEIDNER, CHARLES. (e.c.) San Francisco view publisher plus Panama-Pacific expo views.

WELLMAN, WALTER. (e.c.) New York artist/publisher of suffrage and comic series.

WESTERN NEWS COMPANY. (e.c.) Chicago publisher of presidential portraits set.

WESTERN SOUVENIRS, INC. (l.c.) Rapid City, South Dakota, distributor of regional views.

WHEELOCK, C.E. & COMPANY. (e.c.) Peoria, Illinois, publisher of presidential and state capitol series.

WHITE HOUSE PUBLISHING COMPANY, INC. (l.c.) Cincinnati, Ohio, distributor of regional views.

WILLIAMSON-HAFFNER. (e.c.) Denver view card publisher of Indians, political, state capitols, and western art subjects.

WINSCH, JOHN. (e.c.) New York publisher of greetings and topicals including famous writers and beautiful women; greetings (birth announcements, Valentine's Day, Washington's Birthday, St. Patrick's Day, Easter, Halloween, Thanksgiving, and Christmas), and artist-signed work (Kathryn Elliott, Jason Freixas, Fred Kolb, Charles Levi, Samuel L. Schmucker, and Helen P. Strong).

WIRTH, WALTER. (pio. , e.c.) New York pioneer view card publisher.

WOLF COMPANY. (e.c.) Philadelphia publisher of artist-signed work (Angelo Asti beautiful women, Ellen H. Clapsaddle greetings).

ZERBE, FARRAN. (e.c.) Publisher of wooden postcards.

ZIEHER, OTTMAR. (e.c.) Publisher of philatelic subjects on postcards.

ZIMMERMAN, H. G. (e.c.) Chicago, Illinois, publisher of comics and topicals.

ZORN, FRANK. (e.c.) Sheboygan, Wisconsin, publisher.

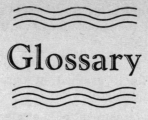

Glossary

Advertising: A category of postcards that advertises a product.

Advertising Trade Card: A precursor of postcards. These colorful and attractive lithographs were given away with household and other products. Some examples of these have been found mailed.

Antique Postcard: Generally any postcard published before World War I.

Approval: A selection of postcards mailed to a customer upon request. The customer may examine and purchase (but is not obligated) any or all of the postcards, but must pay shipping costs both ways. The cards should be paid for or returned within ten days.

Arcade Card: Postcard size, but without a postcard back. These picture cards were usually obtained from a vending machine.

Artist-Signed: The artist's signature is reproduced with the artwork on the postcard.

Auction: Postcards sold to the highest bidder. Bids may be submitted either in person or by mail.

Back: The address side of the postcard. Stamp collectors (philatelists) often think of the address side as the "front" because what's important to them, the stamp and mailing data, appear there.

Chrome, Chrome Era: Today we think of chromes as any modern, glossy-surfaced card. The term "chrome" originated with Kodak's Kodachrome film. Chromes were the first color postcards produced from color film and printed with the photo-mechanical halftone process. We date the beginning of the "chrome era" with the publication of the first series of Union Oil postcards in 1939.

Chromolithograph: Sometimes called "chromo." Reproduction process using finely grained lithographic tones from continuous-tone negatives.

Comic: A humorous treatment of subjects has always been a popular approach on postcards.

Continental Size: Postcards measuring approximately 4 × 6 inches. Most of the postcards published today are continental size.

Current Issue: Contemporary postcards available for sale on retail racks.

Dealer: Person who sells postcards.

Deltiology: The collecting and study of postcards. The word deltiology comes from "delti" (little picture) and "logy" (the theory, science, or study of).

Detroit: Postcard published by Detroit Publishing Co. of Detroit, Michigan. The firm produced thousands of different early view cards by a proprietary lithographic process called Phostint.

Divided Back: Beginning in 1907 in the United States (earlier in Europe), the address side of the postcard (the back) was divided so that a message could be written on half of the space.

DRGM (Deutsches Reichsgebrauchsmuster): Design registered in Germany.

Exposition: Souvenir postcards issued for world expositions and fairs. Those stamped and cancelled on the fairgrounds are particularly sought after, especially by stamp collectors, and may be worth many times the value of an unused exposition postcard.

Fixed Price Sale: Retail selling of postcards at a fixed advertised price.

Front: The picture side of a postcard. (The opposite usage of the term is preferred by philatelists; they consider the address side which bears the stamp, cancellation, and postmark to be the more important and hence "front" side of a card.)

Golden Age (Postcard Era): The period between the Spanish–American War and World War I when the hobby of collecting postcards was at its peak.

Greeting: Postcards mailed as a greeting, in celebration of a holiday or special day. During the Postcard Era, Christmas postcards, followed by Easter postcards, were the most frequently mailed greeting cards. Birthday postcards were also very popular.

Gruss Aus: Literally, "Greetings from." The picture side of many pioneer views contained the words "Gruss Aus" with a location's name and one to three vignetted images of the location joined by loose scrollwork illustrations. A large area was left blank for a message.

Hold-to-Light: Postcard which, when held to the light, glows in certain areas. In die-cut hold-to-lights, the surface layer has been cut away to reveal a thin colored layer of paper through which light can shine. In transparency hold-to-lights, an intermediate paper layer carries a hidden image, visible when held to the light.

Leather: Postcard made of leather. The designs were burned in; sometimes coloring was added.

Linen, Linen Era: Linen-style postcards were widely printed in the United States after World War I when access to quality European printing was restricted by high tariffs. Linens are typically printed in vivid colors on paper with a linen-textured surface, and they tend to have a shadowless airbrushed appearance. The "linen era" extends from the 1920s through the 1950s.

Lot: Postcards grouped for sale as one unit.

Maximum Card: Maximum concurrence of postcard image, stamp image, and cancellation date.

Mitchell: Prolific publisher of early view cards, located in San Francisco.

Modern: Postcard from the past two decades, generally continental size.

Novelty: Postcard made of unusual materials or with attachments, moving parts, or cut-outs. Hold-to-lights and leather postcards are two types of novelty postcards. Other examples are metal attachments or silk clothing attachments.

Old Postcard: While the term is frequently used to mean any postcard older than the person who is talking, a truly old postcard is a pioneer postcard, that is, one produced before July 1, 1898.

PFB: Paul Finkenrath, Berlin, a German publisher of quality postcard greetings.

Philately: The collection and study of postage stamps, revenue stamps, stamped envelopes, postmarks, postal cards, covers, and similar material relating to postal history.

Pioneer: A postcard mailed or produced prior to the effective date (July 1, 1898) of the Private Mailing Card Act of May 19, 1898. The early pictorial images had to be printed on government postal cards to benefit from the postcard rate. Before 1898, images printed on plain card stock required two cents postage. Advertising and views were the most common pioneer postcards.

Postal Card: A card supplied by the U.S. Postal Service, with a postage stamp imprinted or impressed on it.

Postcard: Privately printed mailing card for transmission of an open message at the first-class postcard rate.

Private Mailing Card: A card mailed between 1898 and 1902. The Private Mailing Card Act of 1898 required the following wording to appear on the cards: "Private Mailing Card—Authorized by Act of Congress, May 19, 1898." All private mailing cards could be sent through the mail for one-cent postage.

Real Photo: A picture postcard made directly on photographic paper with a "postcard" back.

SASE or S.A.S.E.: Self-addressed, stamped envelope. Any query which does not include remittance, but where a reply is expected, should be accompanied by an SASE.

Show: Event (convention) where postcards are sold. Ten to 100 dealers may exhibit their postcards in albums and in shoe box-size containers for customers to examine and purchase. A million or more postcards may be available for sale at a large postcard show. In Europe these are called bourses and some American clubs have adopted the term.

Silk: A novelty postcard. There are applied silks where a layer of silk covers part of the picture, e.g., Santa's suit; the image may be printed on silk cloth; the image may be embroidered silk or it may be woven silk.

Standard Size: Postcard measuring 3½ × 5½ inches, oriented either vertically or horizontally.

Stecher: Publisher of quality postcard greetings.

Teich: Postcard published by Curt Teich Co. of Chicago, the most prolific American postcard publisher. Teich views were published from 1898 until 1976.

Topical: The subject of the postcard image, e.g., an animal, a building, an event, or a vehicle.

Tuck: Postcard published by Raphael Tuck & Sons of Great Britain. This firm was the world's largest postcard publisher during postcards' "golden age."

Undivided Back: Postcard published before 1907 (in the United States) when only the address could be written on the back of a picture postcard.

Union Oils: The first chrome postcards in the United States. Series of view cards were published by the (Union) 76 Oil Co. in 1939, 1940, 1941, 1949, 1950, and 1955, amounting to more than 1,000 designs.

Views: Postcards based on realistic images showing people, places, events, and things identified with a specific geographic location.

Whitney: Publisher of postcard greetings.

Winsch: American publisher of quality greetings.

Bibliography

BOOKS

Many postcard monographs are self-published and available only from the author or within the postcard hobby. A bookstore that sells by mail and carries considerable postcard literature is the Gotham Book Mart, 41 West 47th Street, New York, NY 10036.

Austin, Elisabeth K.: *Check List of H. B. Griggs Signed Postcards.* Pawcatuck, CT: Elisabeth K. Austin, 1972.

Banneck, Janet A.: *Rose O'Neill. A Postcard Checklist.* Danville, CA: Janet A. Banneck, 1979.

Budd, Ellen H.: *Ellen H. Clapsaddle Signed Post Cards. An Illustrated Reference Guide.* Cincinnati, OH: Ellen H. Budd, 1989 (1st edition). Over 2,300 Clapsaddle postcard designs are illustrated. This is an indispensable reference for the Clapsaddle specialist!

Burdick, J. R.: *Pioneer Post Cards. The Story of Mailing Cards to 1898 with an Illustrated Checklist of Publishers and Titles.* Franklin Square, NY: Nostalgia Press, 1967 (reprinted).

Carver, Sally S.: *The American Postcard Guide to Tuck.* Brookline, MA: Carves Cards, 1976, revised 1980. Excellent orientation to the world's largest postcard publisher.

Fanelli, Giovanni and Ezio Godoli: *Art Nouveau Postcards.* New York: Rizzoli, English edition 1987. Excellent presentation with illustrations, biographical information, and postcard data for more than 500 artists.

Gibbs, George C.: *The Topographical Locator for Picture Post Card Collectors.* Syracuse, NY: George C. Gibbs, 1987. Lists post offices and branch post offices in the United States, June 1, 1909.

Greenhouse, Bernard L.: *Political Postcards: 1900–1980. A Price Guide.* Syracuse, NY: Postcard Press, 1984.

Grushkin, Paul D.: *The Art of Rock Posters From Presley to Punk.* New York: Abbeville Press, 1987. An important book for postcard collectors because many poster designs were also published as postcards. Filled with illustrations, lists.

Helbock, Richard W.: *Postmarks on Postcards.* Lake Oswego, OR: LaPosta Publications, 1987. A useful guide to the "backs" of postcards used between 1900 and 1920.

Jenkins, Mrs. Jack L.: *The Narrow Hershey Post Cards.* Bloomington, IL: Mrs. Jack L. Jenkins, 1983.

Leler, Hazel: *Winsch Halloween Post Card Check List.* Houston, TX: Hazel Leler, 1982. A carefully researched work that illustrates all known Winsch Halloween postcards.

Lowe, James L.: *Lincoln Postcard Catalog.* Folsom, PA: Deltiologists of America, 1973 (1st revision). Useful as a checklist of postcards on Abraham Lincoln—everything from holiday greetings for Lincoln's birthday to postcards showing streets named Lincoln. Out of date as a price guide to Lincolniana, but useful for relative values.

Lowe, James L. and Ben Papell: *Detroit Publishing Company Collectors' Guide.* First Edition. Newton Square, PA: Deltiologists of America, 1975. A checklist for all known numbered postcards bearing the Detroit Photographic, Detroit Photochrom, and Detroit Publishing Co. names.

McAllister, Ed: *Paul Finkenrath Berlin. P.F.B. Checklist, Topical Guide, Sales Price Range.* Roseville, IL: Colberg Publishing & Printing, 1978, and combined supplements, April 1982.

Megson, Frederick and Mary: *American Advertising Postcards, Sets and Series, 1890–1920. A Catalog and Price Guide.* Martinsville, NJ: The Postcard Lovers, 1985. Packed with data!

Miller, Bonnie P.: *All About DWIG*. Palm Bay, FL: Bonnie P. Miller, Ca. 1965.

Miller, George and Dorothy: *Picture Postcards in the United States, 1893–1918*. New York, NY: Clarkson N. Potter, 1976. The key reference source for early-century American postcards.

Morgan, Hal and Andreas Brown: *Prairie Fires and Paper Moons. The American Photographic Postcard, 1900–1920*. Boston: David R. Godine, 1981. Superb examples of real photo postcard Americana; also useful information on dating real photo postcards.

Nicholson, Susan Brown: *Teddy Bears on Paper*. Dallas, TX: Taylor Publishing Co., 1985. A carefully researched text; includes guide to values for teddy bear postcards and paper collectibles.

Ryan, Dorothy: *Picture Postcards in the United States, 1893–1918*. New York, NY: Clarkson Potter, revised edition 1982. Essentially the George and Dorothy Miller monograph with updated pricing.

Smith, Jack H.: *Military Postcards, 1870–1945*. Greensboro, NC: Wallace-Homestead Book Co., 1988. Interlaces military history with postcard documentation of the military.

———: *Postcard Companion. The Collector's Reference*. Radnor, PA: Wallace-Homestead Book Co., 1989.

———: *Royal Postcards*. Lombard, IL: Wallace-Homestead Book Co., 1987. Pre–World War I royalty postcards, heavily illustrated, plus guide to values.

Staff, Frank: *The Picture Postcard and Its Origins*. London: Lutterworth Press. 1966, 1979 (2nd edition). An excellent work describing the origins of picture postcards!

Stansbury, Kay: *Ryan II and Horina, Too*. Mulhall, OK: Kay Stansbury, 1982.

PERIODICALS

Barr's News. Lansing, IA. A weekly auction newspaper.

Postcard Collector, Iola, WI. A monthly magazine.

OTHER SOURCES OF INFORMATION

MUSEUMS

Curt Teich Postcard Collection, Catherine Hamilton-Smith, Curator, Lake County Museum, Lakewood Forest Preserve, Wauconda, IL.

POSTCARD CLUBS AND POSTCARD SHOWS

Check current listings in *Barr's News* and *Postcard Collector.*

DEALER ASSOCIATIONS

IFPD (International Federation of Postcard Dealers), c/o John McClintock, Executive Secretary, P.O. Box 1765, Manassas, VA 22110. Include a business-size SASE when writing.

Index

DO YOU STILL
HAVE YOUR HEINZ
PICKLE PIN?

The Official® Price Guide to World's Fair Memorabilia is a nostalgic celebration of the 50th and 25th anniversaries of the New York World's Fairs and other fairs around the world!

For the first time, renowned author RICHARD FRIZ, who gave us *The Official® Price Guide to Collectible Toys* and the highly praised *Official® Price Guide to Political Memorabilia,* recounts the history of the World's Fair and examines the extraordinary range of souvenirs and objects created to commemorate these memorable events.

FROM ALL AROUND THE GLOBE, THIS UNIQUE GUIDE WILL LEAVE YOU PACKING FOR THE *NEXT* WORLD'S FAIR!

IT'S A LANDSLIDE!

The votes are in! For the first time in history, here is *the* complete, up-to-date guide to American political memorabilia!

 From Washington to Reagan, memorabilia from A to Z...banners, books, buttons, games, song sheets...they're all here! The *only* guide to give campaign-by-campaign listings and full coverage of items ranging from the women's movement, to prohibition, to other paraphernalia documenting the progress of the American political machine!

THIS IS A WINNER!!

A GALLERY OF
AFFORDABLE ART!

The Official® Identification and Price Guide to Posters, by expert Tony Fusco, showcases these accessible works of art.

- **A graphic journey through design styles from Art Nouveau and Art Deco to contemporary posters.**
- **Advertisements for everything from the theater and movies to the circus and military posters.**
- **Includes sections by leading experts.**
- **Stunning 8-page color insert, *plus* fully indexed.**

This up-to-date, invaluable guide provides an in-depth look at the world of posters!